eating mindfully

SECOND EDITION

how to end mindless eating &
enjoy a balanced relationship with food

susan albers, psyd

New Harbinger Publications, Inc.

Publisher's Note

Distributed in Canada by Raincoast Books

Copyright © 2012 by Susan Albers
New Harbinger Publications, Inc.
5674 Shattuck Avenue
Oakland, CA 94609
www.newharbinger.com

Cover design by Amy Shoup; Text design by Michele Waters-Kermes;
Acquired by Catharine Meyers; Edited by Marisa Solis

Library of Congress Cataloging-in-Publication Data

Albers, Susan, Psy.D.
  Eating mindfully : how to end mindless eating and enjoy a balanced relationship with food / Susan Albers ; foreword by Lilian Cheung. -- 2nd ed.
    p. cm.
  Includes bibliographical references.
  ISBN 978-1-60882-330-7 (pbk. : alk. paper) -- ISBN 978-1-60882-331-4 (pdf e-book) -- ISBN 978-1-60882-332-1 (epub)
  1. Food habits--Psychological aspects. 2. Eating (Philosophy) 3. Awareness. I. Title.
  TX357.A395 2012
  641.01'3--dc23

                                    2012003626

This book is dedicated to my favorite dining companions—
Brookie & Jack.

Author's Note

Shortly after I began working as a therapist, I became mindful of the enormous amount of suffering that hunger, weight, and eating issues cause. This book is my attempt to help prevent further suffering and to provide comfort to those already touched by it. For this reason, I dedicate this book to all those who are struggling to overcome mindless eating. *I wish you the best on your journey to a mindful relationship with food.*

Contents

Part I
mindfulness of the mind

Part II
mindfulness of the body

Part III
mindfulness of feelings

Part IV
mindfulness of thoughts

Part V
mindful eating motivations

Foreword

Food is essential to sustain our lives. Yet our relationship with food in the twenty-first century has become both complex and challenging.

Nutrition science has made major advances over the past thirty years, and we all know that what we choose to eat affects our health and that we can significantly reduce our risk of getting diabetes, high blood pressure, stroke, heart disease, and other debilitating diseases by making healthy food choices. Though nutrition advice in the media can be confusing at times, we are not lacking in science-based information on what to eat to maintain our health.

So, in the face of this broad understanding, the primary question becomes: why do so many people make food choices that can be damaging not only to the their physical health but also to their emotional well-being? The answer lies in our surroundings.

We are living in what many call a "toxic food environment." Sadly, many of us are not fully aware of just how toxic it is—and how it affects us. We are surrounded by supersized and super-processed foods and beverages that we can eat and drink almost anywhere: in the car, at the shopping mall, at our desks.

Scientists are investigating whether these highly processed foods can cause changes in our brains that lead us to devour far more food than our bodies need—a state that some call "conditioned hypereating."

We also live in a toxic media environment. Through televisions, computers, smartphones, and other media, our senses are constantly bombarded with images and commercials driving us to eat more. The assault is unending. The result: we are conditioned to incessantly overeat, overriding our sense of fullness again and again. The media also perpetuates the ideal of thinness, leading us to be dissatisfied with our bodies. This pervasive uneasiness with our size and shape can lead to disordered eating and, potentially, to eating disorders.

Our hectic modern lives certainly don't help us make wiser food choices. The pace of life was much slower before the arrival of the Internet. People did not expect us to reply to their letters within the same day. Nowadays, with e-mail as our major mode of communication, we are bombarded with correspondence with the expectation of a reply within hours, even minutes. Multitasking has become a way of life, and we rarely pay attention to what we eat, how we eat, why we eat what we eat, and how much we eat. In other words, we eat mindlessly.

Stress contributes to mindless eating, and this stress-eating connection is all the more worrisome because the United States is in the middle of a stress epidemic. The majority of Americans experience moderate to high levels of stress, and many people respond to stress by overeating or eating unhealthy foods. Stress adversely affects our whole being, including our immune and cardiovascular systems. It is also associated with depression and heart disease.

What's the culmination of all these societal conditions and trends? The obesity epidemic, with all of its dire health and economic consequences. In the United States, one out of three adults is obese. If the epidemic is not controlled, half of all adult Americans may be obese by 2030. Meanwhile, eating disorders and disordered weight control are common among our youth.

Why is this so alarming? Obesity affects every organ in our bodies. It increases the risks of diabetes, high blood pressure, stroke, heart disease, depression, and other major chronic diseases. Our health care system is already overwhelmed, and obesity may drive it to the breaking point. Furthermore, if we do not turn the obesity epidemic around, this generation of children may have shorter life spans than their parents. Eating disorders and disordered weight control behaviors can also have dire health consequences, such as heart and gastrointestinal problems, osteoporosis, psychiatric illness, substance use, and risk of premature death. As we are now beginning to learn, eating disorders and obesity share similar risk factors—among them dieting, media exposure, and body dissatisfaction—and these similarities are driving researchers to explore whether we can take a broader look at prevention.

What can be done to reverse the worrisome social trends? During the past few decades, public health experts have shifted to emphasize social responsibility for healthy eating. We need to foster healthy communities to ensure that healthy choices are easy choices for all. Yet we cannot ignore personal responsibility, for the simple fact is that what and how much people decide to eat determines their ultimate health status.

One promising solution to keep us on the healthy-eating and healthy-living track while reducing our stress is the practice of mindfulness. Simply put, mindfulness means being completely aware of all that is within ourselves and around us, from moment to moment, without preconceived notions, using a beginner's mind. Mindfulness can be cultivated through meditative practice, and it can also be woven into our everyday lives and actions. People from all walks of life have practiced mindfulness for thousands of years as a way to maintain their health and well-being. Yet scientists have only recently shown increased interest in the effect of mindfulness on health. For example, the National Institutes of Health funded only three studies on mindfulness in 1999. In 2010, it funded over 100 studies. Areas of research include the effect of mindfulness practice on stress reduction, depression, hot flashes, addiction, irritable bowel syndrome, parenting, diabetes, cancer survival, disordered eating, and weight management.

There are ongoing studies suggesting that mindfulness practice can alter the way our brains function, and recent advances in neurobehavioral research support a new framework of weight management based on how brain processes affect eating behavior via the food reward system. This is especially challenging because we are living in an obesity-promoting environment with many opportunities for reinforcing food rewards. Increasingly, experts view mindfulness practice and training of the mind as important approaches that can help people deal with such environments, maintain their healthy weight, and have a healthy relationship with food.

Susan Albers recognized the importance of mindful eating decades ago when she was an exchange student in Japan. She was among the first to introduce the concept of mindful eating to the public when she released the first edition of *Eating*

Mindfully in 2003. Her book offers a lucid and compelling intro-duction to the essential concepts of mindful eating. And it offers concrete exercises that show us how to use mindfulness practice—namely, mindfulness of the mind itself, the body, our feelings, and our thoughts—to transform our uneasy relation-ship with food. We learn how to hear our inner "food critic," how to sort out cravings of the heart from cravings of hunger, and how to break out of the routine of mindless eating. This second edition builds on her extensive experience working with patients and clients. It is a treasure for all of us.

—Lilian Cheung, DSc, RD
Coauthor, *Savor: Mindful Eating, Mindful Life*
Editorial Director, The Nutrition Source,
www.thenutritionsource.org,
Department of Nutrition, Harvard School
of Public Health

Acknowledgments

A noble person is mindful and thankful for the favors he receives from others.

—Buddha

Thank you to New Harbinger Publications for enthusiastically suggesting the second edition of *Eating Mindfully*! I appreciate the opportunity to update readers with the latest mindful eating information and to share many more mindful eating tips. During the past few years, there have been several advances in mindful eating. Since *Eating Mindfully* was published, I've written four more books on how to eat mindfully and cope with comfort eating. I hope to write many more.

I also graciously thank all the readers for their feedback on the first edition of *Eating Mindfully*. If this book touched one life, it completed its mission. I'm happy to say, based on the reader response, that it has touched many. I'm sending you a virtual thank-you for inviting this book into your life and onto your kitchen table.

Thank you to the professionals who are doing research and teaching others about mindful eating. I admire your passion and dedication. Some of these individuals I know personally, others

I've exchanged e-mails with, and a few I have never met but have admired their work from afar. These include Jean L. Kristeller, Ruth Q. Wolever, Evelyn Tribole, Elyse Resch, Michael Pollan, Dean Ornish, Jeffrey Brantley, Jan Chozen Bays, Dr. Jane Goodall, Geneen Roth, Ruth Baer, Jon Kabat-Zinn, Marsha Linehan, Debra Safer, Megrette Fletcher, Marion Nestle, Christopher Garmen, Ellen Langer, Lilian Cheung, Thich Nhat Hanh, Brian Wansink, Jamie Oliver, Mark Bittman, Dr. Mehmet Oz, Dr. Michael Roizen, Ron Siegal, Steven C. Hayes, Zindel Segal, Mark Williams, John Teasdale, and Daniel Siegal. These are just a few people on quite a long list. There are many more fantastic professionals dedicated to helping people transform their relationship to food and embrace mindful eating.

As always, the New Harbinger staff is incredibly supportive and extremely helpful in the process of making my books come to life. They include Catharine Meyers, Earlita Chenault, Jess Beebe, Adia Colar, Julia Kent, Michele Waters, Amy Shoup, and many more.

To those who keep me mindful of family and friendship: Dr. Victoria Gould, Susan Heady, John Bowling, Eric Lingenfelter, Jane Lindquist Lesniewski, Betsy Beyer Swope, Dr. Jason Grief, Dr. Angela Albers, Linda Serotta, Carmela Albers, Dr. Thomas Albers, Rhonda Bowling, John Bowling, and Jim Bowling.

Introduction

How common and effortless it is to eat in an uncontrolled, unaware, *mindless* manner. If you've ever continued to snack when you were full, cut calories despite being hungry, or used guilt to guide your eating, you've experienced mindless eating firsthand. Let's face it. Deciding what to eat is not an easy task. It's so tricky that in the United States eating concerns and weight obsessions have reached epidemic proportions, with serious health, emotional, and economic consequences for a large part of the population. We desperately need something new to help us overcome these issues—and mindful eating might be the answer.

What is mindful eating? A few weeks ago, I discovered an excellent example of it, and the incident involves the best chocolate lava cake I've ever had. You might be wondering how dessert fits into a book about managing your weight and healthy eating. If you want to know the answer, keep reading. Mindful eating, as you will learn in this book, is eating more consciously so you can eat just enough to be satisfied—without eating too much or too little. It sounds simple, but if you've ever tried it, you know it's much easier said than done. Yet, it is an essential skill for managing your weight.

I was at one of my favorite restaurants, a tiny bistro with a menu that changes by season, with a good friend whose name also happens to be Susan. When the waitress arrived, Susan asked to hear the dessert special first. She was interested in the bistro's signature dessert, a warm chocolate fudge molten lava cake. Susan wanted to know, up front, whether the cake was still on the menu because it would impact what she ordered for dinner. If they offered the lava cake, she figured she'd order an appetizer and the cake, no entrée. If not, she'd skip dessert altogether and just order an entrée. She said, "I'm going to *make* room, not *find* room." Knowing this dessert was on the menu helped her choose her meal wisely. She had plenty of room for dessert without feeling overly stuffed. The cake was warm and gooey, and the melted chocolate ran down it like a river.

In general, mindful eating is like this example—learning to eat the things you love in a sensible way. It's breaking old, mindless eating habits and closely gauging your appetite to eat just when you are hungry and stop when you are satisfied. This is a skill that helps you to get to a healthy weight. In this book, you will learn much more about how making simple changes like this can make a big difference to your weight and health.

You may also be wondering what turns an everyday activity like eating into such an overwhelming process. The answer to that question is, of course, a complex one. Throughout this book, we will return to that question with some answers. But the bottom line is this: to make smart, healthy eating choices, your body and mind work together to send you essential cues about what you need and want to eat. These cues give you information about *how much* and *what* to eat. The sensations and emotions that signal when you're full, famished, or just wanting to eat something rich and delicious are a complex combination of bodily and emotional feelings. If you are attentive and responsive to these cues, your eating will be healthier and well regulated.

In this book, you will learn how mindlessness corrupts the way you eat a meal and how it manifests in a variety of eating problems. You will gain insight into why *mindfulness*, which is, of course, the opposite of *mindlessness*, can provide you with valuable skills to control the way you eat.

Welcome

Welcome to the second edition of *Eating Mindfully*! When *Eating Mindfully* was first published, it was among the first mindful eating resources available. Although there were authors and teachers beginning to buzz about mindfulness and its applications to daily life, at the time *Eating Mindfully* was pretty unique. The book examined eating struggles through a different lens— from a new blend of clinical psychology and the ancient wisdom of mindfulness. Having worked with many clients who struggle with eating issues, I wanted the first edition to be very practical and directly applicable to the very real issues people struggle with at the table. Back then, I was excited to apply what I knew of the healing properties of mindfulness to coping with eating problems. Mindfulness was beginning to be used as a treatment for numerous physical and emotional problems. But it had not yet been widely applied to eating. This has changed.

During the past few years, to my excitement, the interest in mindful eating has increased exponentially. It's been on the televised news, in magazines, discussed in newspapers, part of support groups, and embraced by celebrities. In part, mindful eating has received attention due to new research. If you haven't heard of mindful eating yet, that's okay. This book will remedy that by teaching you the ins and outs of eating with awareness. Recently, the Dietary Guidelines Advisory Committee, a group of independent professionals that gives nutrition recommendations to the government, deemed mindful eating to be an effective tool for managing one's weight (see www.cnpp.usda.gov /dietaryguidelines.htm for the latest report). Despite this, unfortunately, many people still have not heard of mindful eating. Given our global concern over healthy eating, eating disorders, and the emotional and physical consequences of obesity, it would be helpful for everyone to know what mindful eating is and how to put it into practice. This book will help accomplish that goal.

What's New in This Book?

The purpose of the first edition was to explain how mindfulness skills could apply to all types of problematic eating. At that time, mindfulness was a new concept to many. Therefore, it was important to start with the basics. The book was written to be a solid introduction to mindful eating. You didn't need any previous knowledge or experience with this concept. However, for those who are familiar with mindful eating, it helped to organize the ideas. No matter where you were in your journey to mindful eating, the first edition could be helpful to you.

Ten years later, the second edition starts with answers to a few of the common questions readers ask most often. Almost all the tips from the previous book are included, and some of the sections have been edited to reflect my evolving understanding of mindfulness. I've also added a new type of mindless eater: the occasional mindless eater. Mindful eating isn't just for problematic eaters or dieters. It's for everyone. Realistically, no one has *perfect* mindful eating. Many people try their best to eat healthfully but experience a bit of mindless eating now and then.

Part V is a completely new addition. It includes fast and easy ways to incorporate mindful eating into your life and is structured as a checklist—you can literally check off the tips as you learn to apply them to your eating regimen. Mindful eating doesn't have to take a lot of time or require radical changes. The new section contains 59 mindful eating tips to help you cope with emotional eating and teach you how to slow down when you eat. Plus you'll find mindful eating quotations that may help motivate you on your journey to mindfulness. There are also many new exercises in each section to help you to become a mindful eater. Finally, there are new resources for finding help and support.

What's Unique about This Book?

If you've read other books on mindful eating, you'll notice that there are several things that are truly unique about *Eating Mindfully*. First of all, this book is totally about you and for you. While I use some personal examples to help illustrate my points and share a bit about myself, this is *not* a book about my eating journey. I want the reader—you—only to be present with your own experience and to be focusing on what works for you. Second, I guarantee that many of the examples in this book will be familiar to you. That's because they are based on real-life struggles that come to my attention every day in my work as a practicing psychologist. The third characteristic that distinguishes *Eating Mindfully* from similar books is that mine is based on the philosophy of mindfulness rather than corresponding spiritual aspects. This concept is based on mindfulness as a way of thinking and living. Being more mindful can help all aspects of your life, not just how you eat.

What Is Mindful Eating?

I used to have a habit of flopping down on the couch every night and watching TV with a huge bowl of pretzels or chips. I would mindlessly munch on my snacks. Halfway through the TV show, I'd suddenly realize that I'd eaten the whole thing! This is when I would get up and go for more. Now, I make sure that I taste each bite.

—Rachel

Among many other things, mindful eating includes feeling the texture of each potato chip on your fingers as you pick it up, and then tasting the salt when you put the chip on your tongue. It's being aware of and listening to the loud crunch of each bite, and the noise that the chewing makes in your head.

When you are eating the chips mindfully, you take note of their consistency against your tongue and the pressure of your teeth grinding together. You feel your saliva moistening the chips and filling the back of your throat, as the chewed food slides down. Mindful eating is feeling the food in your stomach and experiencing pleasure—or whatever you feel—from eating it. When you are watchful, you notice how your stomach expands and feels fuller while you are eating. You experience each bite from start to finish. You slow down every aspect of the eating process to be fully aware of its different parts, and to feel connected to it.

This is only one small example of mindful eating, and many others are included throughout this book. The main message to keep in mind while you read on is that *the key to changing the way you eat is not to develop discipline over your fork but to master control of your mind.* You can do this by studying and understanding your thinking patterns, emotional moods, and various appetites, instead of allowing your old, habitual thoughts to be in control.

Mindful eating is …

- Being aware of *how* you eat.

- Knowing your hunger and fullness cues.

- Sensing and savoring food—truly tasting it.

- Paying attention to the process of eating—for instance, noticing your hand picking up your fork.

- Understanding your emotional triggers—the feelings that urge you to eat or not eat.

- Eating to nourish your body and meet your hunger accurately.

- Adopting a mindful mind-set, one in which you don't judge yourself.

- Being present and aware of your appetite as it changes.

- Having a conscious awareness of your food choices.

- Being alert and observant to how you think about food.

- Letting go of critical thoughts.

- Diligently heeding pre- and post-eating feelings.

- Acknowledging food for what it is rather than categorizing it as good or bad.

- Demonstrating compassion toward self and others.

- Accepting self and body as they are.

Mindless eating is …

- Eating triggered by emotional rather than physical hunger.

- Eating routinely—done in habitual ways.

- Multitasking while eating (watching TV, driving, or talking while consuming food).

- Grazing on food.

- Skipping breakfast or other meals.

- Ignoring hunger and body cues (for example, a rumbling stomach or low energy).

- Continuing to eat despite feeling full.

- Eating everything on your plate regardless of the portion size, a.k.a. being a member of the Clean Plate Club.

- Following the motto "Live to Eat" rather than "Eat to Live."

- Eating for comfort.

- Eating as if in a trance.

- Believing that you have little or no control.

- Allowing the shoulds and shouldn'ts to dominate food consumption.

Shifting Out of Autopilot Eating

At the heart of mindless eating are autopilot actions. Think for a moment about what it feels like to drive on autopilot—and then suddenly experience that wake-up moment when you realize that you've zoned out. It's the shift in consciousness that happens when you are abruptly aware that you've driven to work instead of home or missed your exit. Your hands turned the wheel and your foot pushed the pedal. However, your mind was elsewhere. This shows how easy it is to do even complex things, like driving, with no thought at all. If you can drive on autopilot, consider how effortless it is to eat in this mode. Just pick up your fork and eat. No thought involved.

Unfortunately, behaviors and thoughts that slip out of your awareness are bound to continue and take you places you do not intend to go. Aspects of yourself that are unhealthy can persist without you even knowing it. For example, you might say to yourself automatically, "Eight o'clock, time for a snack." Or whenever you sit down on the couch to watch TV, it's always with a bowl of ice cream. Or maybe you mechanically chomp on cereal right out of the box when you are stressed out. These mindless eating habits are like reflexes. You do them so automatically that eating can be like tying your shoe or brushing your teeth—something you do with little thought.

If you have mindless eating routines, they are going to remain exactly as they are, unless you first become aware of them. When eating habits are in your consciousness, you can begin to think of creative options to change them. You *can* find healthy ways to break out of your old routines.

To Be Mindful ...

At this very moment while you are reading, you are getting your first taste of being mindful. To truly comprehend these chapters, you must shift out of autopilot and attend to the words before you. When you are mindful, you use all of your senses, not just your eyes, to read. You also notice and think about your reactions as you read. Most important, you welcome in what you are reading without judgment.

After the first edition of *Eating Mindfully*, I wrote a workbook to accompany it called *Eat, Drink, and Be Mindful.* I outlined seven skills that can help create a more mindful eater. You may want to keep these aspects of mindfulness in mind as you read this book.

- **Awareness:** Tune in to your senses. Notice. Taste. Smell. Look. Touch.

- **Observation:** See yourself from a distance, as if watching yourself in a movie. Observe the way you eat. Fast? Slow? Small bites? Handfuls at a time?

- **Being in the Moment:** Be in the present moment. When you eat, just eat. Don't worry about the past or the future. You can change only what you eat right now.

- **Letting Go:** Stop holding on tightly to thoughts and feelings that urge you to eat (or not eat). Learn how to let go of an urge or craving without necessarily having to respond to it.

- **Minding Your Environment:** Look around you. Notice what triggers you to eat. The presence of food? Commercials that advertise chocolate to soothe stress?

- **Being nonjudgmental:** Lose the criticism and guilty words. Instead, focus on talking compassionately and kindly to yourself. This will help you to be more honest with yourself about what and how much to eat. Be impartial. Just witness, don't judge.

- **Acceptance:** Be okay with things as they are. Stop fighting with your body and your eating. Instead, listen to your body.

Ten Common Questions about Mindful Eating

Readers have asked many wonderful questions during the past few years, like "I love ice cream. Can I still eat sweets mindfully?" and "What is the best way to start improving my eating habits?" Here are the ten most popular questions on the minds of readers, and their answers.

"If I Start Eating Mindfully, What Will Happen to My Weight? Will I Lose Weight?"

For many people, the answer is "Yes, it's likely that you will lose weight." But, more often than not, I say, "It depends." Let me explain in more detail. When you are engaged in mindless eating habits, you are not meeting your body's needs in some way. It might mean that you are eating portion sizes that are too large, which makes you gain weight. However, if you are dieting or restricting, you aren't getting enough calories or nutrients. This might mean that your body is struggling to maintain a healthy minimum weight.

The bottom line is that this book focuses on improving your eating habits. When you do so, the weight will generally take care of itself. You will notice that this book doesn't hammer in the message "You need to lose weight." The emphasis is more about being healthy than being thin or losing weight. This might mean getting more nutrients or taking better care of yourself. But weight loss can definitely happen as a result of mindful eating. Eating just the right amount needed to make your body function, without giving it too much excess, will allow your body to settle at your natural weight. Ask yourself, when was the last time your body seemed to be at a healthy place—in regard to your weight, health, and feeling good overall?

"Is 'Eating Mindfully' a Diet? What's Wrong with Dieting?"

It's likely that you've already read many diet books. Although this book is about helping you eat better and manage your weight, you may be relieved to find that it is not a new "fad diet." Fad diets, like the cabbage soup diet, no-sugar diet, and low-fat diet, come and go in popularity. Mindful eating is radically different. It's not about cutting out food groups or starving yourself. It is something you do for the long term rather than something you go "on" and "off."

Diets contain rules created for you; they are external pieces of advice. Mindful eating is tuning inward to use your intuitive wisdom to find what works for you. A diet may dictate, for example, that you can't eat sugar. But what happens when it is your birthday and your daughter makes you a birthday cake?

Having a meal plan created by a dietitian is different than a diet. A dietitian helps you develop a well-balanced menu. He or she tailors it to your body's needs rather than you trying to fit into the regulations of a particular diet. Having a professional help you choose healthy foods is a great idea.

Thus, dieting can be incredibly detrimental to your emotional, mental, and physical well-being. Diets can inhibit your ability to accurately decode your body's messages and feedback. The dieting lifestyle is akin to taking a knife and cutting the connection that is your body's only line of communication with your head.

"How Will Awareness Help Me Eat Better?"

Much overeating happens automatically. It can become so routine that you may not even be aware of it. When you start to become more mindful, you begin to see mindless behavior that you hadn't noticed before, like chewing on your fingernails. When someone—or even you, through mindful practice—draws your attention to your reflexive actions, you see it and can start changing the behavior. Similarly, if you aren't aware that you munch when you are nervous, you will stay stuck in this pattern. Awareness can help in the following ways:

- Mindfulness teaches you to be less reactive to stress. In turn, this helps you to reduce emotional eating. Just eliminating emotional eating can impact your weight and health immensely.

- When you are more in tune with your body, you stop eating when you are full and you eat more-realistic portion sizes.

- When you are more aware, you stop automatic behaviors, like picking or grazing on food, that unconsciously lead you to gain weight.

- You notice problematic thinking and feelings about food and how it impacts the way you eat (for example, dealing with guilt and cravings).

"How Does Mindfulness Help People With Different Kinds of Eating Issues?"

Intuitively, it makes sense that mindful eating is helpful to overeaters. It slows you down, makes you more aware of portion sizes, and helps you get out of the negative, automatic cycle with food. So how does it *also* help people who are undereating, or who are chaotic or emotional eaters?

In actuality, mindful eating has been used to treat a wide range of eating issues, from the inability to lose or gain weight to everything in between. There are three main ways that mindful eating works to resolve food-related problems and restore health:

- Mindful eating reconnects you with your body's signals. Whether you are overeating or undereating, you have lost track of your hunger and fullness. Mindful eating plugs you back into your body's cues so you know when to stop and start eating.

- Being mindful brings about better management of your emotions. Sometimes people restrict or overeat as a way to cope with negative feelings. Eating and not eating can distract you from your worries. When you have healthier ways of coping, such as mindful breathing and letting go of anxiety, you no longer manage your emotions through your food choices. You can tolerate your emotions, as uncomfortable as they may be, without pushing them away or stuffing them down with food.

- Mindfulness changes the way you think. Rather than *reacting* to food-related thoughts that urge you to overeat, undereat, emotionally eat, et cetera, you *respond* to them. You can hear these thoughts without obeying them.

These are helpful skills for changing all kinds of eating behavior.

"How Did You Learn about Mindfulness?"

My very first contact with the word "*mindfulness*" happened when I was an exchange student in Japan, as a young adult. I lived with a host family in a little town near Osaka. My host family taught me many things that were unique to me at the time, including the value of being still and being present. While I was in Japan, they took me to many historical sites, including a Zen garden in Kyoto. It was here where I was first introduced to the word "mindfulness." As we sat in the garden, my friends defined the word for me—because one thing that the Zen garden is intended to do is cultivate a sense of mindfulness. Although they described mindfulness in words, I remember very distinctly experiencing it. I shifted from being distracted in my mind to being totally present, sensing the experience to the fullest. After this, we went to other cultural places that brought about the same reaction. We read about mindfulness and discussed it.

That experience changed the way I lived. I learned how to be really in the moment instead of jumping into the future or ruminating in the past. Being truly present translated into being a focused student and learning how to listen. This skill has been invaluable in my relationships with friends and clients.

Fast-forward fifteen years. During graduate school, I learned a lot about eating problems when I worked at various colleges and for eating disorder programs. The word "mindfulness" had become an integral part of my vocabulary. I noticed that I repeatedly used the words "eat mindfully" with my clients. I began describing in detail what I meant by these words. Most people know that the word "mindful" means to be more aware—but this was a particular kind of awareness. I noticed that clients started to say things like "I ate dessert mindfully the other day." It articulated the exact type of relationship many of them wanted to have with food. The objective wasn't to correct overeating or eating too little. Instead, it was learning to eat with awareness—just the right amount.

"Is There Evidence That Mindful Eating Can Help Me?"

Yes! During the past twenty years, there have been many important clinical studies and advances. A good place to begin is by looking at the work of Dr. Jon Kabat-Zinn (2009). His work was pivotal in bringing the concept of mindfulness to medicine. He found a way to systematically research the effect of mindfulness through clinical research. Mindfulness was found to help people cope with a variety of medical problems such as chronic pain, cancer, and psoriasis (Baer 2003; Davidson et al. 2003). Given its success with medical issues, psychologists began to study its application to psychological issues such as anxiety and depression, and particularly to eating issues.

Recent studies have found the following results. Mindful eating can help you to:

- Reduce overeating and binge eating (Kristeller and Wolever 2011; Baer et al. 2005; Smith et al. 2006).

- Lose weight and reduce your body mass index (BMI) (Tapper et al. 2009; Framson et al. 2009; Dalen et al. 2010; Singh et al. 2008).

- Cope with chronic eating problems such as anorexia and bulimia, and reduce anxious thoughts about food and your body (Proulx 2008; Rawal et al. 2009; Hepworth 2011; Lavender, Jardin, and Anderson 2009).

- Improve the symptoms of type 2 diabetes (Rosenzweig 2007; van Son et al. 2011; Faude-Lang et al. 2010).

"What Is the Difference Between Mindfulness of the Mind and Mindfulness of Thoughts?"

The difference between these two notions can be confusing. Both concepts have to do with your brain. But they have different functions. Mindfulness of the mind has to do with your level of awareness. Are you zoned out or very aware of what is happening? Tasting every bite or eating in a robotic manner? Using all your senses to enjoy the experience? Mindfulness of your thoughts pertains to the content of what you are thinking—the stuff that is on your mind. When listening to someone lecture, are you processing what he or she is saying? When eating, are you thinking about your long to-do list? Is your inner food critic sending you messages about what you should or shouldn't eat?

"Does Mindful Eating Mean I Can Eat Anything?"

Yes! You can eat everything and anything. Nothing is off limits. Restriction causes cravings. Period. For instance, if you told yourself that you could never eat your favorite fruit again, you'd be amazed at how much more you'd want it.

One major caveat: although you can eat anything you want, with mindful eating it is likely that you will choose *not* to eat everything. The more you tune in to *what* and *how* you eat, the more particular you become about what you consume. A woman in one of my workshops told me a story about potato chips. She used to love them. Then one day she volunteered to make sack lunches for a school. For an hour, she put potato chips into bags. She recounted how greasy her hands felt at the end of her shift. Her skin was saturated with oil and she couldn't seem to scrub it off. Prior to this, she had never tuned in to the sensation of touching the potato chips. After this, she looked at them in a brand-new way.

Mindful eaters often find fast food less appealing when they are totally tuned in. To their surprise, it begins to taste greasy, artificial, and overly processed. Sometimes mindful eaters' taste buds become more sensitive. They notice when tea is overly sweetened or when cereal is loaded with sugar. They say things like "Oh, that dessert is too sweet." Also, mindful eaters start to review the ingredients in foods to avoid those that are toxic or unhealthy. They realize that their body doesn't feel up to par after eating something full of preservatives or other additives. Whole grains and fruits begin to fill them up and make them feel healthier. Mindful eaters still eat treats and junk food, but in

19

much smaller portions, since even small amounts of sweets and fried foods start to seem like a lot. Thus, your food tastes will likely alter a bit as you become a more conscious eater.

"What Is the Difference Between Cognitive Behavioral Therapy and Mindfulness?"

There are many similarities to cognitive behavioral therapy (CBT) and mindfulness. Both can help you improve your eating habits. For many years, CBT (interventions that target distorted behavior and thought patterns) has been one of the most successful forms of therapy for treating certain eating problems (Zindel et al. 2001). There is a slight difference in how CBT and mindfulness tackle things. Let's say you have a negative thought about food. You say to yourself, "One cookie will make me fat." This is an irrational thought. With CBT you'd recognize this as a negative thought and replace it with a positive, more rational thought, like "One cookie won't make me fat." With mindfulness, you don't replace the thought or try to get rid of it. Instead, you become aware of this thought and accept the thought as it is. When you stop struggling with your thoughts, you can let them go without responding to them with action.

"Do I Have to Have a Spiritual Practice or Be Buddhist to Use a Mindful Eating Approach?"

Mindful eating is much like yoga. Yoga has roots in Buddhism and Eastern meditation. However, it is not necessarily a spiritual practice. Mindful eating and yoga utilize breathing exercises to calm and soothe the body. This is a technique. To eat mindfully, you can adhere to any kind of spiritual background or religion—or none at all. You may notice, however, that you become more relaxed and in tune with yourself through mindfulness. This, in turn, can enhance your spirituality in general, whatever that may be.

How to Use This Book

If you think that you may have some mindless eating habits, keep on reading! You may find it helpful to read through the entire book before attempting any of the skill builders, which are activities at the end of each tip, to help you to put the concept into practice. Remember that some tips may be more appropriate or work better for you than others. Then go back and try out the skill builders that seem to resonate with you.

Make reading be your first exercise in being mindful. As you read, simply be aware of your reactions. Pay attention to your thoughts. Notice when your mind says, "Oh, that is interesting," or when it says, "Hmm, that doesn't sound familiar." Also take note when you get very invested in reading or when your mind starts to wander. Listen when your mind reacts with "I want to try that" or "That exercise sounds really hard." This is useful information. Notice how your mind absorbs all of this information. If your experience doesn't match the examples, or your actions are much more intense, hold that observation in your awareness. You may be ready to try these exercises out now, or you might come back to them in a few weeks. When addressing any kind of problem, people typically are at different stages of readiness to adapt their behavior. So if you don't get started right away, don't worry. You can always come back to begin doing them when you are ready.

Finding Support

I am a strong advocate of finding good support. Sometimes this means joining with a good friend or coworker. But if you feel stuck, you don't have a supportive friend, or you have been struggling for a long time, it is important to join with a professional like a therapist, physician, or dietitian—or all three. This book is not a substitute for professional counseling. However, it can be a valuable adjunct to ongoing treatment if that is something you need.

If you make an appointment with a therapist or doctor, make sure to look for someone highly recommended. Seek a professional who specializes in eating problems. Bring along your copy of *Eating Mindfully* and discuss the concepts and skill builders together. It may be helpful to talk about which exercises work for you and which do not. Working together with a professional, you may be able to pinpoint the factors that have been standing in the way of mindful eating. There are several good resources to help you find qualified professionals; see the Resources section at the back of this book for more information.

Perhaps you've been reluctant to make a counseling appointment. Maybe you feel that you should be able to do it on your own, without intervention. Remember that even with a counselor, the greatest portion of the work is still up to you. Also, seeking help does not signify failure and is not a sign of weakness. I cannot emphasize this enough. I admire the strength and courage it takes to seek assistance. It means you care about yourself, and it is a sign that you believe there is something inside of you worth nurturing and protecting. Seeking guidance indicates that you want to live the fullest life possible, and you are willing to take another human being into your confidence to ensure your life will be a happy one. This is a mindful stance, nonjudgmental, open, and receptive to all experience. This is the stance that this book will encourage you to adopt, and, I hope, these chapters will provide many tools for you to do just that.

The Four Foundations of Mindfulness

Imagine for a moment that you are holding a bowl of chicken noodle soup. Think about grasping the steaming bowl in your hands. Picture yourself bringing a spoonful of the liquidy noodles to your mouth. Let's think about what happens in your mind as you begin to imagine this scenerio. It's likely that you immediately had an emotional reaction to the words "chicken noodle soup." Maybe it reminded you of a chilly, snowy day. Perhaps your mind drifted back to when you were a kid and sick with a cold. You may have wondered whether soup was something you craved. Your taste buds may have sprung into action, anticipating the salty warmth heating up your body. The point is that eating isn't just about picking up the spoon and putting it into your mouth. It's a lot more complex. Just thinking about eating creates an entire body, mind, cognitive, and emotional reaction.

The mind-body reaction to food is reminiscent of a story I studied in Japan about Buddha and the four foundations of mindfulness. This story, along with my clinical work, set the basis for how this book is organized. It's linked to important aspects of Buddha's teachings, the four foundations of mindfulness—being mindful of your mind, body, thoughts, and feelings, which you will notice are the very same four factors that impact the way you eat.

As a young adult, Buddha discovered that mastering mindful eating was essential to his spiritual growth. He had been born into a royal family and, when he was a child, he always ate the most succulent and richest foods that India could offer. He grew plump from all of the feasts he consumed. As a young man, he discovered that all the pleasures he enjoyed at the court could not ensure happiness or protect against sadness. So when he left his royal life to seek enlightenment and a cure for suffering, he tried fasting. He discovered that fasting or severely restricting his food consumption made him weak, ill, and unable to concentrate, and it brought him no closer to solving the enigma of suffering. What did the Buddha learn from his days of feasting and famine? He learned that both too much and too little food are detrimental to health and well-being. Balance and understanding the unique needs of your body are essential for a happy, healthy life. As you can see, eating issues have been around for a very, very long time. Even Buddha struggled with balancing his eating. It took time and practice. However, Buddha eventually mastered the concept of mindful eating. He found a balance between eating too much and eating too little. This allowed him to get back to his work. The four foundations are outlined by the Buddha in the *Mahasatipatthana Sutta (The Great Discourse on the Four Foundations of Mindfulness)*.

It sounds easy enough to just "be more aware" of what you eat. But mindful eating is much more complex and sophisticated than that. It's understanding *why* and *how* you eat, the factors that make you stop and start eating. The four foundations can help you answer those important questions. Sometimes you are very aware of how you feel about food—for instance, you know you love the taste of chocolate. But other times it is more unconscious—eating chocolate may subconsciously stir up a lot of guilt. When you eat mindfully, essentially you bring all of the unconscious, buried forces that dictate how you eat to the surface so that your mind can examine them, and you can begin to see how thoughts and feelings impact the way you eat.

Each of the first four sections of this book explores in detail one of the four foundations of mindful eating, and each provides exercises for being conscious of the impact your mind, body, thoughts, and feelings have on your eating. These skill builders are contemporary ideas tailored to help mindless eaters create a contemplative awareness of the four foundations, as they relate to food. When these four foundations remain unconscious, they have an inordinate amount of power and influence over the way you feed yourself.

The four foundations of mindful eating are as follows:

Mindfulness of the Mind

It's difficult for me to know when I should or need to eat. So many things sway my eating habits. At work, I eat snacks my coworkers bring in just because the food is there and I don't want to be rude. At other times, I don't reach for a second helping because I'm wondering if other people are secretly snickering about my weight. I've learned to step back and really ask myself, "Am I hungry at this moment?"

—Emily

Mindfuless of the mind includes becoming aware of many aspects of your mind and your level of attention. At any given moment, your mind can be distracted, restless, sleepy, clinging to the past, zoned out, obsessed, scattered, vigilant, or guarded, among many other ways of being. These states are transient, changing from moment to moment, but all the while they create a backdrop for understanding how you eat. Here are ways you can be more conscious of what is happening in your mind:

- Be more aware of sensations (hear, taste, touch, smell, see).

- Notice whether you are mindlessly munching or tasting every bite.

- Be aware of what your mind is doing (obsessing, worrying, craving, etc.).

- Be in the moment, focused on what is happening right now.

- Pay attention to how your hunger and fullness change with each bite.

- Break out of autopilot eating habits.

Mindfulness of the Body

My body tells me when I'm hungry and full. If my stomach is grumbling, it's my body's way of saying, "I am hungry," and I know I've waited too long to eat. If I overeat, my body complains that it feels sluggish, bloated, and uncomfortable. I listen carefully and respond to my body's requests the first time it asks. I pay attention to what makes my body feel content and energized.

—Molly

Body mindfulness is attending to every aspect of your inner and outer body. It includes paying attention to your hunger and fullness cues. It's noticing how it feels to open and close your mouth when you chew. Tuning in to your breathing and body through yoga and meditation are also key. Examples of how you can be mindful of your inner and outer bodily sensations:

- Pay attention to the process of eating, like picking up your fork.

- Be attentive to your breathing, which can relax your body and move you into the moment.

- Tune in to body sensations, such as your feet touching the floor or clothing rubbing your skin.

- Taste and savor food, noticing the texture and flavor.

- Hear hunger cues, like a rumbling stomach.

- Understand your satiety and fullness cues.

- Relax your body to help alleviate stress.

- Meditate and practice yoga.

- Notice how your body moves—how you walk, sit, run, et cetera.

Mindfulness of Feelings

I often find myself seeking comfort foods that deceptively take away my stress almost immediately. When I am mindful, I opt instead to meditate on what prompted me to seek the comfort in the first place. I acknowledge that a candy bar will make me feel good now, but I also consider how my mood will shift into guilt mode later. I don't allow my feelings to be in complete charge of what I eat.

—Andrew

Mindfulness of feelings involves naming and embracing your feelings, whether they are positive or negative emotions. Food and feelings are tightly interwoven with each other. Being mindful of your emotions helps you to know what feelings trigger emotional eating and/or stop you from eating well. Things to keep in mind:

- Be aware of feelings that prompt you to eat, like boredom, stress, pain, or loneliness.

- Be aware of the feelings that follow eating, such as pleasure, satiation, or comfort.

- Notice emotions linked with overeating, such as shame, sadness, guilt, and regret.

- Pay attention to feelings that come from eating mindfully, like feeling energized, satiated, content, or comfortable.

- Notice where you feel emotions in the body. For example, some people feel sadness as a hole in the belly. They overeat to fill the perceived hole. To others sadness feels as if their hearts are being squeezed. Some people feel anger as a kind of electrical current coursing through their bodies, while to others anger feels like heat radiating from the chest.

Mindfulness of Thoughts

I am most critical of myself inside my head. I might be smiling as I take a second muffin, but my head is saying, "You can't eat that, you're already too fat." When I am mindful of my thoughts, I examine them more closely to see which beliefs are realistic and which ones are just created out of irrational thoughts, judgments, and feeling insecure about how I look.

—Heidi

Mindfulness of your thoughts means being mindful of the content of your thoughts—what you think and say to yourself. Your thoughts can be like subliminal audiotapes that your mind plays over and over, without your conscious awareness that they are playing. When you are mindful of your thoughts, you hear what you think without necessarily acting on it. Here are ways to practice this:

- Raise your awareness of your internal stream of thoughts about food and hunger.

- Notice how thoughts impact your hunger and fullness (such as "I'm so full" or "It looks so good" or "I'll start my diet tomorrow").

- Be aware of your inner critic.

- Tune in to the dialogue in your head that says, "You shouldn't eat that" or "Don't eat that."

- Notice black-and-white thinking (such as believing that a food is either healthy or unhealthy).

- Use compassionate language instead of judgmental words.

- Notice types of thoughts—judgments, dreams, beliefs, negative, positive, catastrophic, black and white.

Mindfulness in Everyday Life

Mindfulness is a way of thinking and being in the world that is many centuries old. It is defined generally as *being present and engaged in each moment in a nonjudgmental way*. It's adapted from Buddhist practices of meditation. If you've done any kind of yoga or relaxation, it's likely that you've experienced aspects of mindfulness.

There are many ways in which you can be more mindful. Eating with greater attention is just one way. You can be more mindful of how much money you spend. Or you can be more present in relationships. Perhaps you see parents at the playground distracted by their cell phones instead of being really present and playing with their kids. Maybe you don't really listen when your significant other is telling you about his day. Our attention can be very scattered and distracted by so many things.

The term "mindfulness" came into use in the sixth century during the Buddha's lifetime. When Buddhism spread across Asia and adapted to the customs and needs of many different countries, the practice of mindfulness remained a core concept. The continued use and popularity of mindfulness exercises today attests to their timelessness and to the value of its healing power. Mindfulness promotes physical health, rehabilitation, and healing, as well as being a treatment for mental health problems (Baer 2003).

Today, in the West, the mind-body connection has been well documented and extensively researched. It is no secret that healing and treating the mind is as important as nursing the body to health. Mindfulness is currently used in conjunction with medical treatments for illnesses such as cancer, AIDS, anxiety, stress, and depression, as well as for chronic pain and sleep problems.

The biological underpinnings are simple. When struggling with an illness, your body's defense system uses all of its resources to target the problem. When you feel pain, either emotional or physical, your natural tendency is to fight against your distress. However, denying and resisting aches and pains raises your stress level and uses energy resources that could be used instead to heal the origin of the illness.

Instead of fighting the pain, mindfulness treatments teach you how to be aware of painful sensations and to manage them one moment at a time. For example, suppose you are suffering from back pain. Instead of being angry or irritated by it, you can observe the source, watch it, and target the painful areas with specific relaxation exercises. When you are stressed and emotionally in pain, your body's natural immunity decreases. If you are stressed out about your weight or your out-of-control eating, you may spend more of your time reacting to and dwelling on the painfulness of your problem rather than dealing with it directly.

Insight is one of the most valuable gifts that mindfulness can offer. When you focus on the here and now, free of distraction, you are empowered to make decisions and free to explore new paths to happiness.

A mindful perspective suggests that healing begins by acknowledging and compassionately accepting that something in your life is causing you grief. This stance has helped people get through extraordinarily difficult conditions that at first seemed to be overwhelming and beyond control. So if you have felt that changing your eating habits is too difficult, know that this approach can help you manage that feeling and move past it.

What Kind of Mindless Eater Are You?

This book is for all those who have issues with their weight or who feel unable to control what they eat—that is, all those who eat mindlessly. The following broad categories describe five types of mindless eaters: *the occasional mindless eater, the chronic mindless dieter, the mindless undereater, the mindless overeater,* and *the mindless chaotic eater.* These catagories are not meant to be a diagnosis but a way of identifying similar habits.

This book encompasses the entire range of mindless eating. The breadth of this approach is one thing, among many, that is so exciting and unique about mindful eating. Everyone can benefit from it, from the person who mindlessly eats only once in a while—like at a restaurant where there is something he really craves—to the individual who has been wrestling with her eating for twenty-five years and feels stuck. Thankfully, this is also a great approach for people who have struggled with dieting. Approximately 33 percent of American men and 46 percent of American women are on a diet (Bish et al. 2005; Kruger et al. 2004). By tomorrow, the majority will give up and need something healthier to replace their eating habits. Essentially, this book is for everyone.

New in this edition is the introduction of the occasional mindless eater. This category acknowledges anyone who succumbs to mindless eating from time to time. The occasional mindless eater generally eats mindfully. However, he may experience mindless eating on a stressful day, at restaurants, or during the holidays. Though infrequent, these occurrences of mindless eating are still bothersome to those who experience it.

If the characteristics discussed in the following sections seem familiar to you, it is likely that you are experiencing some form of mindless eating. It should be emphasized, however, that everyone is unique. People may demonstrate similarities in their eating habits, but the specific characteristics and expressions of mindless eating are shaped by your life experiences, culture, and family. Therefore, you need not identify with every characteristic listed. What is more likely is that you will identify with some aspects of each type of mindless eating. Again, keep in mind that the categories below are not meant to be a diagnosis but rather a way of grouping certain kinds of eating patterns.

The Occasional Mindless Eater

As a child, Jill didn't think twice about what she ate. She ate everything—pizza, tomatoes, bananas, doughnuts. You name it, she would eat it. In college, her eating habits were like many other students'. She ate pizza almost every day and sometimes ate cereal or ramen noodles for dinner because they were cheap and convenient for a student without a lot of money. After college, Jill noticed that her tastes began to change. She became more strategic about her meals. It was important to her to try to create balanced meals of green vegetables and a main dish. It didn't always work, but she did her best. She cut down on sweets and began to consider how food impacted her health. Jill struggled with migraine headaches. Eating well was one thing she could do to help prevent them.

Jill tries to eat pretty healthy day to day. And, for the most part, she is pretty successful at it. But mindful eating slips on occasion. She notices that it happens mostly when she is stressed out at work. As soon as she gets home, she begins rummaging around the kitchen looking for something sweet. It doesn't happen very often, but when it does it bothers her. Jill also struggles on holidays when there are so many good sweets around. She keeps few treats in her home. When she sees them at parties, she tends to eat more than she wishes she would.

Everyone eats mindlessly on occasion. It's pretty normal. For the most part, you eat reasonably well.

Characteristics of the Occasional Mindless Eater

Mind

- Mostly aware of how much she eats but slips up from time to time

- Occasionally enters into trance-like eating, often when stressed or tired

- Being aware of portion sizes becomes a challenge around favorite foods

- Sometimes very surprised that she has gained weight because she is generally tuned in to her body and eating

- Tends to lose track of eating when out to dinner with friends who eat mindlessly

Body

- Generally stays at a pretty consistent weight; if weight gain happens it is very slowly or in spurts

- May notice changes in her body during the holidays or vacations

- Tends to feel overly full when eating at restaurants

- Is vulnerable to overeating new things or comfort foods from childhood

- Is generally tuned in to hunger but occasionally can lose track of it when busy

Thoughts

- Is vulnerable to automatic thoughts like "Oh, I'll start my diet tomorrow"

- Thinks about what to eat but may slip into habitual or routine ways of eating when overwhelmed

- May think guilty thoughts after overeating

- May be critical of herself when she eats too much

Feelings

- Typically uses healthy activities to feel better but occasionally eats for stress relief

- May overeat when feeling extremely anxious or nervous

- Gets frustrated when she overeats because it generally isn't a problem

- May use food to celebrate or be social

The Chronic Mindless Dieter

After her first baby was born, Alex gained fifteen pounds. She tried each new fad diet that came along and hunted for new dieting tricks to "get skinny." In the two years after the baby's birth, she bought no new clothes. She wanted to wait until she had shed ten pounds and could fit into a smaller size. She dreamed about having a flatter stomach and wearing a sexy little black dress. She was no stranger to eradicating sugar, fat, and carbohydrates from her diet. Sometimes she even fasted. On one "miracle diet," she ate nothing but cabbage soup and lost a few pounds, but she was unable to maintain the weight loss.

The worst aspect of these diets was that they were completely unrealistic in terms of her lifestyle. When she reduced her carbohydrate intake, she could no longer bring a sandwich to work for her lunch. Furthermore, she found she couldn't live without pasta and bagels. If she took the fat-free approach, she ate more food and felt less satisfied. She also had difficulty finding fat-free food that wasn't filled with sugar or salt to cover the taste.

No diet made sense, and she was always falling off the wagon. When she jumped back on, other people complained that they couldn't invite her to their homes because they never knew what food would be appropriate to serve to her. Moreover, her conversation about dieting was obsessive and boring. She constantly criticized herself when she "cheated" on her diet.

Characteristics of the Chronic Mindless Dieter

Mind

- Vigilant about food intake, scrutinizes food labels

- Categorizes food as "good" or "bad"

- Makes food choices based on hoped-for weight loss, rather than on health

- Eats a lot before starting a diet and believes the diet will last for only a short time

Body

- Engages in yo-yo dieting, leading to constant body-weight increase and decrease, which in the long run is very unhealthy

- Is perpetually dieting and tries out all the new weight-loss gimmicks

- Fasts and cuts back food intake to unhealthy levels

- Doesn't listen to his body's desires

Thoughts

- Knows a lot of information about calories, food portions, and diet tricks

- Ignores nutrient needs

- Believes he has an "ideal" weight to achieve

- Talks and thinks about food frequently

- Thinks more about the caloric value of food than the experience or joy of eating

Feelings

- Feels fat; disapproves of, and/or is disgusted with his own body

- Experiences mood fluctuations based on eating behavior

- Experiences guilt when he "breaks the diet"

- Examines other people's bodies; frequently checks mirrors

- Feels as if he cheated when he eats something that is not part of his diet

- Has difficulty accepting the shape of his own body and wishes for someone else's

The Mindless Undereater

Fiona's eating issues began in the seventh grade. As the first girl in her class to reach puberty, she endured extensive teasing about her breasts and rapidly changing body. She wore baggy clothes to avoid others' comments and to focus attention away from her curvy shape.

As a young adult, Fiona obsessed about eating. She refused to put milk in her coffee if it wasn't fat-free, and she used artificial sweeteners in her cereal to avoid the ten extra calories in real sugar. Eating a handful of chips could send her spiraling into a whirlwind of guilt for the rest of the day. Because she believed that other people evaluated and judged what she ate, she found it particularly painful to eat in front of others. Her friends and relatives constantly nagged her about looking too thin. They even acted like the "food police" and would tell her what to eat. Regardless of what everyone said about how "painfully thin" she was, she continued to feel fat and did not enjoy eating.

Characteristics of the Mindless Undereater

Mind

- Restricts food intake or eliminates entire food groups such as all red meats, cheese, or wheat products

- Engages in food rituals or has strict, repetitive habits for eating; for example, eats only frozen meals or eats at the same time every day

- Has a strong desire for perfection

Body

- Experiences a significant drop in body weight

- Has a slow metabolism (her body burns food very slowly)

- Experiences a variety of physical consequences, such as a decrease in heart rate and body temperature and loss of menstrual cycle

- Is drowsy most of the time, has difficulty concentrating, has low energy

Thoughts

- Preoccupied with appearance

- Feels fat or has a negative body image

- Has an unrealistic perception of her own body

- Determines self-worth by weight

- Engages in inflexible and extreme either-or, black-or-white thinking

- Makes constant critical judgments about weight and self

Feelings

- Feels fat; disapproves of, and/or is disgusted with her body

- Experiences intense mood fluctuations based on eating behavior

- Experiences guilt when she breaks the diet

- Examines other people's bodies, frequently checks mirrors

- Feels as if she "cheated" when she eats something that is not part of her diet

- Has difficulty accepting the shape of her own body and wishes for someone else's

The Mindless Overeater

Jessie described herself as a chubby kid. Other children on the block nicknamed her "Chunk." In her home, food was an extremely complicated issue. Her grandfather, a Holocaust survivor who had experienced the effects of forced starvation, encouraged her to eat as much as possible. Her Italian mother's expression of love was to prepare frequent, large, elaborate meals. In general, the family sat around the dinner table in silence. They ate much more than they talked.

As an adult, Jessie was constantly trying to eat "normally." She described her hunger as "ravenous" and "insatiable." She hoarded cakes, bags of cookies, bagels, and ice cream. She promised herself to eat these foods only for dessert or as a snack. But she could eat an entire cake in one night, without batting an eye, and she often did just that. Eating one cookie was dangerous, because she felt unable to stop until she finished the entire bag. Her eating was "good" unless she had a difficult day at work, after which a late-night binge helped her cope and not dwell on feelings of inadequacy. Of course, following the binge, she would feel terribly guilty about all of her overeating.

Characteristics of the Mindless Overeater

Mind

- Knows that his eating is out of control

- Believes that he is unable to stop eating

- Experiences intense food cravings

Body

- Eats more than is considered "average" during a set period

- Eats, chews, and swallows very rapidly

- Increases or shifts in weight frequently

- Has high blood pressure, fatigue, trouble breathing, high cholesterol level, et cetera

Thoughts

- Is cognizant of fullness but continues eating anyway

- Avoids scales or discussions of weight or weight loss

- Believes that weight is tied to success and failure

- Engages in supercritical thinking about self and weight

Feelings

- Feels distress over bingeing behavior

- Feels embarrassment that leads to eating small amounts of food when in public, but large amounts when alone

- Feels like a social outcast because of being overweight

The Mindless Chaotic Eater

Sam first recognized the severity of his mindless eating patterns when confronted by his roommate, Jim. Jim discovered that Sam stole his food and binged on his stock of candy bars whenever Jim left the apartment. To hide his thefts, Sam would run to the candy store to replace the stolen items. He hoped his roommate wouldn't notice that he took the food, but then he was caught.

When Sam gobbled up the candy bars, he knew he should stop, but he just kept shoving candy bars into his mouth. After eating an entire box of candy, Sam always felt awful. He ended his binges by making himself throw up or by exercising intensely.

He was afraid to get into a relationship for fear his partner would discover his eating problems. In his last relationship, his partner frequently became angry and tried to make him stop eating so chaotically. Sam ended the relationship because he had lost the ability to know which foods or people were good or bad for him.

Characteristics of the Mindless Chaotic Eater

Mind

- Purchases large amounts of food that are eaten secretively

- Overeats, then purges (via vomiting, overexercising, laxatives, and/or diuretics)

Body

- Experiences extreme fluctuations in weight

- Purges food—pays lengthy visits to the bathroom after eating excessive quantities of food

- Exercises excessively

- Purchases large quantities of food, diuretic drugs, and/ or diet pills

- Has unusual swelling around jaws

- Experiences negative body reactions, such as gastrointestinal problems, bloating, gas, headaches, and/or sore throats

Thoughts

- Thinks about self very critically and negatively

- Experiences self-worth as determined by weight

- Engages in rigid thinking

Feelings

- Experiences intense mood swings

- Fears being or becoming fat

- Doesn't cope well with stress and anxiety

- Feels temporary relief after purging

Now that you have identified what kind of mindless eating you may be pertinent to you, let's get started. It's time to learn the art of mindful eating.

Part I

mindfulness
of the mind

*The secret of health for both mind and body is not to
mourn for the past, not to worry about the future, and not
to anticipate troubles, but to live in the present moment
wisely and earnestly.*

—Buddha

#1
Awareness: Awakening Your Mind

"Well," said Pooh, "what I like best," and then he had to stop and think. Because although Eating Honey was a very good thing to do, there was a moment just before you began to eat it which was better than when you were, but he didn't know what it was called.

—A. A. Milne, *The House at Pooh Corner*

The first step to being mindful is to become more *aware*. While it sounds simple, it is a much more difficult task than you might imagine. You might think that you are very conscious—maybe even painfully aware—of how you eat. But mindfulness is a special kind of awareness. It's not just about bringing things into your consciousness but focusing your attention and senses in a special way.

Let's say, for example, that you are aware that you are eating a cinnamon roll. Being mindful encompasses much more than that realization. It's turning your attention to how you eat the roll. Fast? Slow? It's noticing the shape of the pastry, smelling the cinnamon, and feeling the sticky sugar on your fingers. It's the taste of it on your tongue. It's also observing any feelings that pop up when you eat it: guilt, pleasure, longing, warmth. And finally, it's paying attention to the thoughts that are playing in your mind as you eat, such as worrying about calories and cravings. Maybe it makes you think about your mother, who used to make cinnamon rolls on Sunday morning. Just reading about a cinnamon roll at this very moment might make you salivate. Clearly, we have very intense mind-body reactions to food.

The good news about developing this type of awareness is that it doesn't take a lot of effort or time. It does not require any actions or major changes. Instead, it merely advises you to reorient where you place your attention and your mental focus. Using your five senses can help you to cultivate this kind of mindful awareness. When you first become aware of an object, there is a brief instance of pure awareness just before you identify what it is. That happens when your awareness jumps to alertness via your sense of sight, smell, sound, taste, and touch.

Holly described an example of becoming more mindful. At first, Holly changed nothing about the way she ate. Instead, she just paid special attention to her eating habits. Holly, one of my clients, noticed that she did a lot of mindless munching, or zoning out, between the time she opened a bag of pretzels and finishing the last few bites. She didn't remember much about the taste or how much she ate in between. Paying attention to the juicy smell of a freshly cut apple or the crunchy texture of granola made her snacking more pleasurable, and she became more in charge of how much she ate. This, in turn, gave her much more satisfaction. Holly didn't have to make any drastic changes to her diet or employ restrictions to become a more mindful eater—she simply paid more attention.

Skill Builder: *Mindful Bites*

The following is a classic mindfulness exercise. Mindful eating begins by slowing down and awakening your senses while you are eating. All you need is a comfortable, quiet space and a handful of sunflower seeds (or raisins, or a single cookie). Place the seeds in your palm. First, become aware of their color and shape. Silently use words to describe to yourself what you see. Compare and contrast each of the seeds. See the shadows, indents, and patterns in their outer skins. Notice their weight and texture against your skin. Do the seeds feel light, heavy, rough, or soft? Do they have regular, consistent shapes and sizes, or are they all different? Next, move some seeds between the tips of your fingers. Feel their edges and shapes and the sensations they produce in your fingers. Contrast this with how you remember them feeling in your palm. Now move the seeds up toward your face and smell them. Observe what comes to mind when you take their odor into your nostrils. Do they bring to mind a memory or an image? Next, close your eyes and place the seeds in your mouth. Think about what it feels like when you run your tongue around the seeds. As you chew the seeds, do you begin to salivate? Are they crunchy? Observe and describe the taste. Is it sweet, salty, or bitter? What do you hear? Notice the sound of your jaw rotating to chew and the sound of your swallow. Say the word "seed" in your head. Repeat it several times before you swallow. What is the sensation as the chewed seeds slide down your throat?

Skill Builder: *Awakening Your Senses*

This exercise also helps you access and observe your raw sensations—what you see, hear, and feel. It can be extremely helpful when you are angry or feel overwhelmed by what's on your mind. Strong emotions often make it difficult to stay with pure sensations and just be aware. Here is what to do:

1. Notice the ebb and flow of your breathing. Relax. Move around to settle yourself. You are learning how to train your mind to attend only to what is happening in the moment. Start with your vision. Say to yourself, "I see ...," and observe what you see around you. Identify colors, shapes, and contrasts in hues and textures. Close your eyes and reproduce what you saw as an image inside your mind's eye. Move on to what you hear. Say to yourself, "I hear ...," and describe the sounds around you.

2. Continue on to what you smell, taste, and touch.

3. This exercise incorporates one more sense: your feelings. Say to yourself, "I feel ...," and label your feelings. You can feel conflicting emotions simultaneously. For example, you can feel both happy and sad in the same moment. Remember to stay at the level of sensation. Try not to analyze or interpret.

This exercise is intended to reconnect you with basic, raw physical sensations. Feel what your hands are touching, attend to what you smell, acknowledge how your body feels in its position. Observe the color of the walls around you and the details of an object nearby.

#2
Observing What's on Your Mind

He who distinguishes the true savor of his food can never be a glutton; he who does not cannot be otherwise.

—Henry David Thoreau

Consider *how* you think about food. Do you daydream about cake? Obsess over calories? Plot how to get junk food? Ignore cravings? Push thoughts of chocolate out of your mind when you are on a diet? Your mind is constanly swirling and chattering about food. It is hard to slow down and observe *how* you think about it.

The mind is like a river, constantly changing directions. It can move quickly from gently flowing to raging out of control. At any given moment, you are thinking, dreaming, scheming, calculating, processing, and contemplating. These are just a few examples of the many complex things your mind can do.

Observing is just *seeing it like it is, without judgment or alteration.* Try thinking of observation as being like painting a picture of what's going on in your head. While painting this picture, you don't add an extra dab of paint to make your thoughts look better, or erase parts you don't like. Nor do you paint it the way you think it *should* look. You simply paint what is inside your head, without judgment or commentary. Do the same with observing your thoughts about food and eating.

When you observe, take a mental step back. The vantage point should be from a distance rather than from right in the middle of the experience. This is like watching yourself on a movie screen instead of being one of the actors in it. You can also think of it to be like looking at your mind from above, as if your brain was a pot on the stove: take the lid off, peek inside, and see what's stewing in your mind.

Lori used observation skills to change the way she ordered food at restaurants. She was incredibly frustrated by how long it took her to make a selection. To stop the behavior, she became aware of her indecision and turned on her watchful mind to observe what stood in the way of a simple decision. Lori said, "I noticed when I was negotiating. I wasn't just thinking about satisfying my hunger, I was *bargaining* with myself. I was saying things like, 'If I don't order the hamburger, I can have a candy bar later. If I have chicken, then I can order soup as well.' I didn't judge or criticize myself for doing this. After observing my bargaining strategy, I concluded that the wisest choice would be to stop negotiating and focus on what would be most satisfying and nourishing. Which I did."

Skill Builder: *Observe Your Hungry Mind and Your Full Mind*

To do this exercise, conduct a mind experiment. Simply observe what happens inside and outside of yourself when you *are* hungry as opposed to when you *are not* hungry. This might mean when you are full, but it could also just be when you are satisfied, neither hungry nor full. Notice and describe as much detail as possible. Observe thoughts, feelings, and what you sense in your body. You may want to do this exercise again at various states of hunger and fullness—when you are a little hungry, very hungry, and starving. Try it at different times of the day.

Observing the Hungry Mind: These are some of the activities in which the hungry mind engages: planning how to obtain food, craving, desiring, dreaming about a snack, feeling scattered and unable to concentrate, feeling unsatisfied, being distracted by smells, listening intently for coworkers leaving for lunch, watching the clock.

Write down in a notebook or digital journal how your mind thinks when you are hungry.

Observing the Comfortably Full Mind: These are some of the activities in which the comfortably full mind engages: feeling satisfied, being able to focus on work, feeling happy, feeling soothed, feeling content, feeling warm, feeling at rest, being attentive, being aware, thinking about things other than food or guilt. You may find that feeling full may bring up a negative feeling. If so, that is okay; just take note of it.

Write down in a notebook or digital journal how your mind thinks when you are full.

#3
Moment-to-Moment Eating

The way you cut your meat reflects the way you live.

—Confucius

Let's imagine that you are sitting at your kitchen table eating a salad. Now picture yourself touching your fork. Next, visualize picking up the fork slowly and piercing a piece of lettuce. Imagine bringing this leaf up to your mouth and placing it on your tongue. Eating a mindful meal means focusing your mind on the process of eating.

Think for a moment about the way you eat. Do you pop food into your mouth without a second thought? Or thoughtlessly pick at food left on your plate even after you are done? Do you finish the entire bag once it is open? Do you put only one type of food on your fork at a time? Do you cut each bite into small pieces? How you eat can contribute to mindless eating, particularly when your patterns are unconscious and automatic.

Moment-to-moment eating has many benefits. It can make eating more enjoyable. This is how you truly savor food. It also can help you avoid bingeing and overeating. Mary constantly worried that her cravings would lead to a binge. She had been down that road many times. Often when she indulged in just one chocolate chip cookie, she felt that she had lost control and had eaten too many.

To ease her worries, Mary used mindful eating skills to slow herself down. When she gobbled up cookies, she didn't really enjoy them as much as she thought she would. So she practiced paying attention to and savoring the sweet, rich taste, the mouth-watering smell, and the soft, melting texture of the cookies. When she was really in touch with these sensations, eating was pleasurable and more controlled. Taking it one moment at a time helped prevent her from entering into an eating trance, whereby she would consume food without really thinking about it or tasting it.

Skill Builder: *Slowly but Surely, Decelerating Your Eating*

On your mark, get set, go! Starting a meal can sometimes feel like you have entered a running race. You might find that you race quickly through your meal. Or you might discover that you're a sprinter, with short bursts of speed, making for an uneven eating pace. Instead, aim for a slower, steady pace. When you reduce your speed, you can be more present and in charge of your portion sizes. Here are some simple ways to slow down:

- **Switch hands.** Place your fork or spoon in your non-dominant hand and eat with it. This will help shift you out of autopilot eating.

- **Turn your fork upside down.** People in England turn their forks down to stab their food and pick it up. As Americans, we scoop with our forks. The simple act of scooping can lend itself to mindless eating.

- **Use your senses.** If you find that you are eating too quickly, shift into mindful mode by focusing on all your senses—hearing, seeing, smelling, tasting, feeling. Choose one aspect of the food to focus your full attention on. For example, smell your food. Before each bite, intentionally inhale deeply for a moment.

- **Chew, chew, chew.** Take a small bite. Set a chew-per-bite ratio (it will vary by what you are eating).

- **Take one bite at a time.** Tell yourself, "Stay with this bite." Notice whether your mind wants to push you on to the next bite before you have finished this one. Don't go for another bite until your mouth is completely empty of this bite.

- **Eat with small utensils.** A baby spoon and a shrimp fork will naturally slow down your pace and help you to take smaller bites.

- **Create an intermission.** Establish a break during eating, like you would experience during a play between acts. During that time, take a drink. Or commit to putting down your fork and telling a short story or getting up for a minute.

- **Pace yourself.** Runners often can't tell how fast they are going without concrete clues like a clock or keeping up with another runner. Use your dining companions to help you understand and set your pace. Notice who is eating the fastest and slowest. Aim to eat in conjunction with or slower than the slowest eater at the table.

- **Put your fork down for a moment.** Take your hand away. Place it in your lap. Then begin to eat again. Notice how uncomfortable it may feel to remove your hand from your utensil.

- **Set the ambience.** Try playing slow music that your body can move in sync with.

- **Ease into it.** Maybe you can't turn on a dime from the rush-rush of daily life. If you find this really challenging, just commit to taking one slow bite.

Skill Builder: *In-the-Moment Meals*

You can try out moment-to-moment eating by paying attention to the entire process.

- **Be aware.** Start by looking at your food, noting the different colors and shapes—the vivid red of a tomato to the smooth and silky texture of yogurt. Watch your hand reach for the spoon or fork. Pay attention to how quickly you do this. Acknowledge grasping and lifting a knife and cutting meat. Notice how it feels when you open and close your mouth. Be alert to how you chew, the temperature of the food, the taste. Acknowledge what you hear, such as the food sizzling, the crunching noise that chewing makes, the sound produced by slurping through a straw. Continue to notice each sensation, right through swallowing. This is moment-to-moment eating.

- **Try chopsticks.** One way to slow down the process of eating is to challenge the way you've always done it. Try eating a meal using a pair of chopsticks instead of your customary utensils. This will force you to take smaller portions, eat more slowly, and look at your food more closely. Touch the chopsticks, feel your fingers flex and grip them, and describe the experience to yourself. At first, you may have trouble picking up the food. Stay with it. Keep trying.

- **Create a gap.** Observe the gap between each bite. If you struggle with a habit of picking at your food, closely watch your hand leave the plate. Notice the gap in space and time that exists between your hand leaving the plate and it moving toward your mouth and touching it. Fill that space with a mantra ("Eat, drink, and be mindful!") or a choice ("I decide where my hand will move next"), or just pay attention to how quickly your hand moves.

- **Play "I Spy."** Play "I Spy": cup your hands in a circle, look through them like you are peering through a telescope, and look down at your plate—just see one bite at a time.

#4
Balancing What You Eat with How You Eat

Becky started a food diary. She wrote down everything she ate including how many calories she consumed. Becky winced every time she had to write down something she considered a "mistake" or "cheating." She didn't want to share those entries with her dietitian, so she quit after just a day or two. She knew the diary would be helpful but couldn't seem to get herself to do it.

Many weight management programs encourage you to record what you eat. This is nothing new. However, traditional food logs often ask you only to keep track of the serving size and the calorie content. A mindful food diary is much different. You write down many different dimensions of eating. For example, you explore what you were feeling before and after you ate. Then you take note of what you were thinking at the time. You also assess your hunger level and how your attention shifted as you ate. Overall, keeping a mindful food diary helps you to become much more *aware* of *how* and *why* you are eating.

Here is an important caveat before you get started. Be sure to use a compassionate voice. If you judge what you eat, it's unlikely you will write it down; you may avoid keeping a record of what you eat altogether. If you want to start a food diary, but seem to struggle with it emotionally, you might prefer to take a step back to work on compassion first (see #11, The Compassionate Mind).

Skill Builder: *Be Mindful of the Four Pillars*

Start keeping a mindful food diary. Record everything you eat every day for several weeks. If tracking foods and specific details increases your anxiety or obsessiveness, just track how eating affects each pillar—your mind, body, thoughts, and feelings. Remember, this is to help you to become more aware and in tune with your eating habits. While it may be an investment of time now, later you'll become much better at keeping track in your head alone. When that day comes, you may no longer need to record anything on paper or digitally.

If you would like help creating a mindful eating journal, you can purchase the Eating Mindfully app. Type in your meals or snacks, or snap a picture. Then, record how it affects your mind, body, feelings, and thoughts. There is also a mindful hunger scale to help you determine if you are eating because you are physically hungry or to fill an emotional need. Finally, you can set the alarm function to chime to remind you did mindfully during a particular time of the day.

Here is an example of an entry in a mindful food log:

My Mindfulness Food Diary

Breakfast: Muffin, Orange Juice, Banana

Mindfulness of Mind: I felt really hungry this morning. I didn't have much to eat last night. I have a lot of demanding things to do today. It was hard to stay focused on eating. I may need to pay more attention to my hunger when I'm really stressed out.

Mindfulness of Body: My body felt better after eating this breakfast. I know I should bring a snack to work for 10 o'clock, because this won't be enough to carry me through to lunch. At this moment, though, I am not hungry, and I don't feel stuffed. I feel just right.

Mindfulness of Thoughts: I noticed that my critical self appeared again and questioned whether I could really afford to eat the muffin. Then I had an argument in my head. I reassured myself that it was okay to eat the muffin. I also checked in with my body, which felt fine.

Mindfulness of Feelings: The muffin was great. It was crumbly and sweet, and it made my mouth water. I noticed feeling that I was doing a bad thing because I was taking such pleasure in the muffin. Overall, though, I felt good about eating it, and I let go of the worry.

Keep this kind of record for an entire day to document every meal and snack you eat. Then try to keep a food diary for a week, two weeks, a month. You will get a very clear picture of your eating patterns and habits, which will be very helpful to you on your journey toward eating mindfully all the time.

#5
Mindful Meals:
Contemplating Food

When a popular fast-food chain proposed opening a restaurant at the base of an ancient landmark, the Spanish steps in Rome, there was an enormous outcry from the community. Why did they mind so much? Italians are famous for their lengthy, leisurely meals. The presence of a fast-food restaurant threatened this cultural stance on eating. Eating is an experience. It is not to be rushed or done on the fly. American culture often emphasizes the extreme opposite of leisurely dining, inherent in the term "fast food."

The "slow food movement," which is common in European countries, is a way of eating and living that honors food. It celebrates the process of eating and savoring food. Thankfully, it is becoming more popular in America and around the world. It connects enjoying food with a commitment to taking care of the environment.

While the idea of savoring food is becoming more popular, it may still feel very new and difficult to put into practice. Slowing down can feel like a foreign concept. Multitasking, or doing several things simultaneously, seems like a much more efficient way to get things done when you are busy. For example, you might talk on the phone while cooking, or read a book while in class. Eating is an activity performed so automatically that you may find yourself surfing the Internet, reading the newspaper or a blog, talking, watching TV, and listening to music at the same time as eating.

While multitasking appears to save time, doing it while you eat has some major downsides. Research shows that dividing your attention between eating and another task, like watching TV or listening to the radio, increases the likelihood of overeating (Hetherington et al. 2006). Eating in front of the TV, for example, increases intake by 14 percent, while talking to a friend can increase how much you consume by 18 percent. Basically, doing two things at once can inhibit your concentration and awareness. This impairs your ability to choose foods wisely. In the extreme, splitting your attention can be dangerous, as in the case of trying to wrestle a sandwich out of a wrapper while you drive. However, for undereaters, who need to eat more, distraction can be used for your benefit: eating while watching a movie or during social events can increase your consumption without you overthinking it or being hypervigilant about calories.

Alex's eating habits were strongly dictated by convenience. She preferred anything that she could grab while she was walking out the door. She ate at her desk or in the car. Taking a more mindful approach began with a simple action—just sitting down in one place when she ate. Then she put food on a plate instead of eating it right out of a fast food bag. Rather than answering her e-mails and phone messages during lunch, she committed to doing one thing at a time. When she ate, she just ate. She focused on the act and process of eating.

For the first time, Alex really tasted her lunch. Her brain and stomach were able to register the fact that food had entered her body, and they sent her a clear message when she was full. She made fewer careless mistakes on her work that were the result of dividing her attention between working and eating. Best of all, she was more conscious of how much she ate rather than just finishing the portion size given to her.

Skill Building: *Mindful Meals*

Start with one mealtime: breakfast, brunch, lunch, or supper. Choose a specific location to eat, such as at your kitchen table or in the lunchroom at work. Sit quietly in that area, and don't allow any distractions. Place all the food you intend to eat on the table before starting so you don't have to get up. Don't answer the phone if it rings. Put away the newspaper, turn off the TV, stay away from your e-mail. Just eat. It may feel uncomfortable at first. As you do this exercise, pay attention to what you think, how you enjoy your food, and the amount you consume.

Skill Builder: *Zooming In*

Put a loose rubber band around your wrist. When you feel that your mind is wandering or that you are not truly present, snap the rubber band lightly. This isn't to cause pain but to tap yourself lightly with a new sensation. If you are eating and seem like you can't stop, you can try this technique. The aim is to move you into the *now* and to get you out of a mindless eating trance.

Skill Building: *Mindful Walking*

Mindfulness teachers traditionally assign their students to do a walking exercise. This is meant to demonstrate the value of channeling the mind onto one activity only. You may wish to try it. This can give you good practice at doing one thing at a time. You may want to pick one sensation to focus on. Students are instructed to notice how they walk, their pace, the movement of their legs, the sounds around them, and their feet hitting the ground. The exercise teaches the students not to think, just to walk and observe. By analogy, if you are eating, just focus on the process of eating and enjoying your meal.

#6
Minding How You Eat

Imagine for a moment that you have a handful of nuts in your right and left hands. In your right hand, the peanuts are in the shell. In your left hand, they've been taken out of the shell. Consider how quickly you would eat the peanuts in your left hand versus your right. It's not an easy task to get the peanuts out of their shell. It's likely that you could eat the entire handful of shelled peanuts in a matter of seconds—before you even get the first peanut out of its shell.

If you love nuts but steer clear of them because you are afraid of eating too many, the good news is that you don't have to avoid them anymore. Sometimes changing *how* you eat something, like peanuts, can make a big difference. Eating nuts from the shell gives you a great opportunity for learning mindful eating.

Dr. Jim Painter and several colleagues at the School of Family and Consumer Sciences at Eastern Illinois University found that subjects offered in-shell pistachios consumed an average of 125 calories. In the second part of the study, subjects offered pistachios removed from the shell consumed an average of 211 calories (Kennedy-Hagan et al. 2011). This constituted a difference of 86 calories. What's interesting is that the participants rated their fullness and satisfaction the same despite the fact that one group ate more (Honselman et al. 2011). Keep in mind that a mindful approach isn't obsessively concerned with the calories. Presenting these numbers is meant to quantify the difference, not to urge you to cut down on calories.

Thus, simply buying pistachios in their shells will help you to eat them more mindfully. Why? Because it takes time to remove the pistachios from their shells. This reduces the tendency to pop them mindlessly into your mouth. Anything that naturally slows you down will help you to be more in charge of your portion size. While that study focused on pistachios, other nuts and foods would likely have a congruent result.

Another study by the School of Family and Consumer Sciences showed that people who kept the shells in sight versus throwing them away consumed an average of 216 calories (Kennedy-Hagan et al. 2011). The other half of the people threw out the shells. These subjects consumed an average of 264 calories, a difference of 48 calories. They termed this the "Pistachio Effect." This means that just looking at a pile of pistachio shells can significantly reduce the total number you eat, since it helps you to remember how many you already ate. Without this visual cue, you can really underestimate or forget how much you ate.

Skill Builder: *Using the Pistachio Effect*

Keep visual cues of what you eat. This can help you to be aware and more conscious of how much you eat. The pistachio effect principle also is applicable to many other foods. A cup, candy wrapper, or snack bag left on your desk is a good visual reminder of what you've eaten or drunk. It's very easy and normal to forget what you've consumed when you have many things to remember. So the next time you have a craving for nuts, it may be worth taking a scoop of nuts that are in their shells. It's nice when a snack food can assist you to naturally and easily eat more mindfully.

#7
Emotional Categorizing

In the sky, there is no distinction of east and west; people create distinctions out of their own minds and then believe them to be true.

—Buddha

Do you sit in the same seat at the dinner table for each meal? Eat the same cereal every single day? Snack in front of the TV at the same time each day? Inflexible eating routines are a common cause of mindless eating. On the upside, habits and repetition help to simplify the world. They make the overwhelming decision of choosing what to eat pretty simple and quick. You make more than 200 decisions every single day about what to eat and not to eat (Wansink and Sobal 2007). It's no wonder you can get so exhausted by it! The downside is that habits don't force you to consciously think through each and every decision. You get stuck doing the same thing over and over again.

A common habit is to categorize food based on emotions. This means that you may look at a food and automatically think, "Too fattening" or "That brownie is bad!" Other feelings-based categories might be "safe" or "unsafe," or "good" or "bad," or "I like it" or "I don't like it." Categories can be problematic when you typecast a food in a mindless, automatic way. In other words, you decide that you are going to eat it based on what arbitrary category you've placed the food in rather than many other factors, like whether it tastes good, is healthy for you, and so on. The thought process is like this: "That meatball sandwich is bad, therefore I can't have it." Emotional responses like this are crippling to mindful eating because they place rigid boundaries around food that aren't necessarily intrinsic to that food. So be wary of categorizing food based on your feelings. Start to pay attention to whether you make choices based on emotional reflexes or dieting restrictions rather than by mindfully tuning in.

Amy believed she ate in a healthy manner, until she took a conscious inventory of her food consumption. Amy ate a pretty rigid menu. It consisted mostly of salad, bagels, and other "diet foods." Although she loved a wide variety of foods, she ate these diet foods because they were low in fat. They were on her safe list—not too many calories or fat. If she ate only these things, she didn't have to make many decisions. Amy automatically said no to things like cheese and certain meats, because she had read that they have high fat contents. Even avocados were placed in the automatic-no category, even though they are healthy in many ways.

Creating emotion-based food categories had allowed Amy to eat without much guilt or thought. However, she became extremely bored with what she ate. More important, it reduced her intake of crucial protein, vitamins, and minerals. Thinking that she "couldn't" and "shouldn't" eat various foods began to prey on her mind. Having few options made her angry. It was draining to want something from outside her limited menu and yet say no just because it wasn't on the safe list. This made eating no fun.

Skill Builder: *Understanding Emotional Food Categories*

Try the following exercises to help you truly understand the nature of categorizing:

- **Test your categorizing response.** Go to your cupboard right now. Take out the first thing you see. Pick it up. What are the thoughts and emotions that come to mind when you look at it: "Yum" or "Yuck"? "I love this food" or "No way I'd eat this—it's too fattening"? "Bland" or "Tasty"? "Safe to eat" or "Not on my safe list"? Pay attention to your very first gut reaction. What emotional category do you place this food in? What other labels do you attach to it? Now pick up another food and repeat. Doing this exercise will show you how automatic your reactions are to food. These gut reactions, in part, dictate whether you eat something. At your next meal, notice how your mind sorts and organizes food.

- **Stop categorizing.** This is an important mindfulness skill in general, not just for food. Placing things in categories is a judgment. It also closes your mind to possibilities instead of opening it. For example, notice when you call a food "good" or "bad." Remember that the food itself in not inherently "good" or "bad." It's what you do with the food that is important. Do you savor it or mindlessly munch on it? It's true that some foods are healthier than others. But instead of labeling them "good" or "bad" or putting them in emotion-based categories on the "safe" or "unsafe" lists of your diet, think of these foods as being on a continuum. A tomato is on the healthier end of the continuum whereas fast food may be toward the opposite end. A continuum allows you to respond more flexibly to these foods.

- **Check your food rules.** Listen closely to your thoughts about restrictions you put on food. Write them down. Notice whether you follow these rules automatically with little or no thought. These food rules may be part of what is keeping you stuck. If, for example, you tell yourself, "I can't eat snacks in the late afternoon," realize that following this rule may make it difficult to keep your hunger in check.

- **Remove the "bad" label from treats.** You can do so by giving a cookie a *purpose* or *function*. Think through *why* you might eat it. Is your intention to have a snack? Are you eating it for a treat? To relieve stress? Because you are hungry? If it is a treat, eat the cookie in mindful bites, or use it to satisfy a craving for sweets. Or give yourself a prescription for a once-a-day dose of a cookie.

Skill Builder: *Shake Up Your Routines*

Break out of your standard routine. Whether you go to the grocery store and buy the same items week after week, or zoom down the aisles looking for the specials, do something different. Examine and buy an exotic fruit like a mango, a papaya, or an Asian pear. Or try a loaf of artisan whole-wheat bread. Add a touch of spice and variety to your meals. Walk through the store mindfully examining each item. Be aware of products you've never noticed before. Touch and turn over packages, smell the fruits, examine everything, and try a new food.

#8
Sitting Still with Your Pain

Endurance is one of the most difficult disciplines, but it is to the one who endures that the final victory comes.

—Buddha

If you've picked up this book, it's likely that you know how tough eating can be. Food has probably caused you a lot of grief in one way or another. Perhaps you've been unable to sleep at night because you were starving. Or you couldn't get anything done because you felt so guilty for eating too many helpings of mashed potatoes. Trying to balance your eating habits with feeling good about your body can be incredibly taxing on your mood and cause a lot of emotional pain—frustration, hopelessness, fear, et cetera.

Buddhist philosophy talks a lot about suffering. The desire to escape suffering is the deep emotional root of many issues, particularly mindless eating. Interestingly, eating (and not eating) can cause pain, but it can also distract from things that are bothering you (Heatherton and Baumeister 1991). When you eat, maybe your mind isn't thinking about paying the bills or your awful boss. When you are really hungry, your mind focuses on wanting food, not your rocky relationship with your significant other. Therefore, sometimes you may eat just to avoid feeling uncomfortable or sad.

Rachel called on the lyrics of Kenny Rogers's song "The Gambler" to describe how she hid from her fears and never knew when to face them. She felt that identifying exactly when to "hold them," "fold them," "walk away," or "run" wasn't her strongest skill. That is, she had trouble deciding when to run from danger and when to stand her ground and confront her fears.

If you aren't a fighter, your natural strategy for surviving in the world may be to flee or freeze in place. Arguments, pain, conflict, difficult projects, and anxiety can be very hard to tolerate. When you are mindful, you don't run from life, even from those things that are most painful. Accept experience as it is, as hard as that may be. Sometimes the places you go to escape cause more problems than the place from which you started. For example, if you avoid fixing a flat tire, you may ruin your entire car instead of having to just fix the tire.

One way to be mindful is to welcome in every experience, even those that are difficult. It sounds odd. But the point is to make the fear less scary and less in control of you. Tonya, for example, entered therapy to discuss her fear of sexual intimacy. She had developed a suspiciously repetitive dating pattern. When the relationship became physical, she quickly backed away. A mindful approach urged her to examine what she was mindlessly running from in each relationship. As it turned out, it wasn't sex she feared but being self-conscious about her body. She feared that her body would not be attractive to, and would therefore be rejected by, the men she dated. Tonya was a healthy, desirable weight, but she was still grappling with her emotions and her critical self-judgments. It wasn't dating or finding the right guy that was the problem. Instead, her discomfort with her body was what was truly standing in the way.

Skill Builder: *Sitting with Uncomfortable Feelings*

Stress eating is a way of pushing away your emotions. Food numbs and distracts you. To counter that, try to "feel the feelings." This means to stay with the uncomfortable feeling without soothing yourself with food. When you have the urge to stress eat, get one piece of hard candy, like a butterscotch or a peppermint. Commit to sitting still and sucking on the candy without chewing on it. It will take a while for this piece of candy to dissolve in your mouth. Notice what is happening in your mind as you wait for this piece of candy to melt. Identify the specific feeling that is driving you to stress eat. When it is completely and totally dissolved, reevaluate how you feel. Ask yourself if you still feel like stress eating. If so, repeat again with another candy.

Skill Builder: *Unclutter Your Mind Meditation*

In this exercise you will try to embrace rather than push away any issues that you may be avoiding when you eat or don't eat. Take a few moments to sit still. Maybe it is when you are sitting quietly in your car or before you go to bed at night. Ask yourself if there are any feelings, thoughts, or problems you are trying to escape or avoid. Have you put something aside, hoping it will just get better gradually, without any input from you? Sort through the issue you don't like to think about. Do this by imagining your mind as your desk. When you sit down at a cluttered desk, often the first impulse is to clean it. Putting papers into neat piles, eliminating clutter, and creating space foster a sense of relief. Facing your problems rather than avoiding them is like making your messy desk manageable instead of finding another place to sit.

What does your mind look like? What is the messiest area? Do you stuff clutter and bad feelings away in a drawer? Are you obsessed with order? Accept whatever feelings arise. They might be anger, frustration, or pain. Try not to think of ways to fix it, just acknowledge whatever you feel and sit still with the feelings. Set aside your desire to change the things that trouble you, and just examine what is cluttering up your mind.

#9
Living in the Now

Do not dwell in the past, do not dream of the future,
concentrate the mind on the present moment.

—Buddha

Where is your mind right now? Are you thinking about the future, telling yourself, "I will start eating better tomorrow." Or maybe your mind is the past thinking, "I can't stop regretting eating that third slice of pizza!" When you are mindful, your mind is focused on *right now.* It's easy to become trapped in memories from the past and fantasies about the future. These two mind-sets entice you away from being truly present in the moment. The consequence is always thinking, "I should have" or "I can't wait until," rather than "I am right here, right now." Stay aware of this truth: the present moment is the only *real* time you ever have. You can't change the past or control the future, *but you can impact what you are eating right now.*

Contemplating the past can be helpful when the purpose is to understand and know yourself better. Reflection is most helpful when it is done with an accepting stance and the desire is to learn from the past rather than to change it. For example, you might look back at your food log to understand why you tend to snack at night.

Many mindless eaters have had more than their share of painful past experiences. They may have experienced bullying

81

about their weight as a kid or scathing comments about their body from a parent. Not surprising, such memories are likely to be ever-present in the mind, consciously or subconsciously. Such memories can draw you away from the present and tempt you to live in the past, mentally reworking what you "should have done." If this is true for you, it is important to work on treating and healing your pain so that you can enjoy living in the present.

Skill Builder: *Living in the Present*

In this exercise, you will learn one type of Buddhist meditation for letting go of the past and living in the present. It is called *dhyana* meditation. It slows down your mind to prevent you from jumping from one thought to another.

In this exercise, choose a thought that often interferes with your ability to live in the moment. It could be a recurring thought about your appearance, or a mistake you made, or an unkindness you experienced. It could be a repeating thought about anything.

Next, imagine a stream flowing down the side of a grassy hill. Picture yourself sitting by the side of the stream watching leaves and twigs float by. You can think about your mind as if it were a flowing stream. Thoughts, like leaves, constantly float by. At the bank of the stream, you can stop the leaves and pick them up out of the water, or you can watch them float by you. You can do the same with your thoughts. You can pick one out of your many thoughts and dwell on it, or you can let it float by with all of your other thoughts. Notice when negative thoughts about yourself or your body come into your awareness. Don't react to them. Instead, you can take note of their presence and let them float right by you. If you have a negative thought about your past, picking it up and dwelling on it can trap you in the past and prevent you from living in the moment. If you must reach for that thought, hold it briefly, then visualize tossing it back into the stream. Let it go.

#10
What's on Your Mind?
Not on Your Plate!

To conquer oneself is a greater victory than to conquer thousands in a battle.

—Buddha

Tina told a compelling story about how difficult it was to cope with her fear of a small, protruding growth on her belly. Terrified that it was cancer, she did not go to the doctor. After two years, the benign growth had expanded so much that it weighed close to ten pounds. If she had addressed the problem early on, it could have been removed by a simple, virtually painless surgical procedure. But letting it grow for as long as she had caused numerous other health problems, nearly insurmountable emotional issues, and social isolation. None of these issues were caused by the growth itself. They were the result of not attending to it. Tina finally had to have extensive, invasive surgery to remove it. Had she continued to ignore it, eventually it would have killed her.

In a way, we all carry around a type of noncancerous growth: the issues that aren't big at first, but the longer we avoid dealing with them out of fear, the faster they grow and the more they weigh us down. Facing some pain in the present can forestall much bigger pain in the future. Addressing a weight issue, or any other problem silently expanding in your body or your psyche, will lighten your mind and heart.

Madison struggled with her eating for many years. She gained a lot of weight quickly and was unable to alter this despite many efforts. For her, gaining weight was a form of protection. As a young adult, she was sexually assaulted. Subconsciously, she believed that being overweight would prevent men from being interested in her, so she wouldn't have to face dealing with the assault. This eventually evolved into another problem: the over-eating of food.

Like with Madison, sometimes food is only part of the issue. It is just the visual manifestation of other concerns. Food is a very easily obtainable, legal, and constantly present substance. It can numb you and provide temporary soothing and comfort. Also, unlike drugs and alcohol, food is a more socially acceptable drug and emotional anesthetic. Consider whether you are eating to numb other worries in your life.

Eating is something people have to deal with every single day, which makes it one of the most difficult undertakings to alter. Unlike using alcohol or drugs, which you can cut out from your life entirely, you cannot stop eating food. Eating mindfully means learning how to fine-tune your food consumption, not how to eliminate it.

Mindless eating problems are like icebergs, because it is very hard to see how deep they go and what they hide. The "tip of the iceberg" is the visible aspect of your food consumption: how many times a day you eat, the specific types of foods you consume, and the quantity. But the real question of why you eat what you eat is invisible and can be answered only by exploring within yourself—by examining the unseen part of the iceberg beneath the surface.

Skill Builder: *The Issues Beneath Mindless Eating*

Visualize a large iceberg in the middle of the Arctic Ocean. Presume that the "tip of the iceberg" represents what, when, and how much you eat. To find out *why* you eat, you must dive under the freezing waters to see the core of the glacial mass.

What's under the iceberg? Make a list of any problems that may be festering and triggering eating problems, such as stress, feeling overwhelmed, anger, et cetera. If you can't name what these triggers are, that's okay. Just be watchful of your reaction and emotions around food. Start being attentive to what feelings trigger emotional eating—fear, pain, loss, rejection, hopelessness, stress, anxiety, and the like—or any type of eating that isn't precipitated by physical hunger.

Remember that turning away from the issues below the surface can be hazardous and leave you vulnerable to unpredictable, hidden dangers. The *Titanic* sank because of a large portion of the iceberg that lay below the surface. Don't let unexamined emotions rock your boat.

#11
The Compassionate Mind

If you want others to be happy, practice compassion. If you want to be happy, practice compassion.

—Dalai Lama

What do you say to yourself when you've eaten past the point of being full? If you struggle with eating, you are familiar with how easy it is to lack compassion for yourself. When you've eaten too many cookies, it's hard to be forgiving and say kind things to yourself. In fact, you might call yourself "bad" or "weak" (or even harsher names!) for eating mindlessly.

A key component of improving your eating habits is changing the way you talk to yourself. Self-criticism and name calling are the polar opposite of compassion. It may seem counterintuitive. You might think to yourself, "But won't I just mindlessly eat again if I am kind to myself? Doesn't this just give me liberty to do it again?" But beating yourself up with criticism only makes you feel worse and can prompt more mindless eating. The cycle goes like this: overeat, feel bad, criticize yourself, feel bad about yourself, eat to soothe yourself, repeat. Compassion, on the other hand, stops this cycle by helping you examine the entire sequence of events rather than judge it. Compassion is very different than allowing or excusing behavior.

In Buddhist teaching, people are instructed on how to be compassionate—that is, to show respect and love to every single living entity. Since you are a living entity, being compassionate

87

also means having empathy for yourself. Compassion includes having patience, generosity, tolerance, and forgiveness not only for others but also for your own struggles. Compassionate behavior also means letting go of envy, spite, critical attitudes, and the desire for revenge. These elements of compassion are integral aspects of living in a way that does no harm—to others or to yourself. They are fundamental Buddhist principles for living well.

Buddha emphasized that *you yourself, as much as anybody in the entire universe, deserve your love and affection*. No matter who you are, you need and have the right to be treated well. You cannot treat yourself well if you are not gentle and compassionate with yourself about your own issues.

Skill Builder: *Being Mindfully Compassionate*

Speak to yourself with compassionate rather than harsh words. Buddha instructs us that *one word that brings peace is better than a thousand hollow words*. Remember that compassion helps you to think deeply and honestly about what triggered an episode of mindless eating.

If speaking kindly to yourself is foreign to you, imagine the words you would say to a small child. When you start getting down on yourself, counter critical thoughts with statements like these:

It's okay; next time, it will be easier.

I really do try hard, but I had a really tough day.

It's not my fault. Let's try again.

It's a struggle to be mindful when I feel this way.

I understand; I know this is hard.

Everyone makes mistakes.

I am in pain about this, but it will pass.

Being mindful is a process; it takes time.

I want what is best for me.

I love and accept myself—no matter what happens, or what I do.

#12
Dealing with the Blues Mindfully

Linda came home at six o'clock every evening, stressed out from cold-calling prospective customers. Even before she took off her coat, she walked directly to the kitchen. She grabbed anything that was within easy reach to cram into her mouth. There were many days when she devoured a steady stream of pretzels and dry cereal until dinner was ready. Then she ate dinner. One day, as she walked into her apartment, she got a phone call. She sat down, took the call, and then sat there thinking about her day. Two hours passed before she ate.

Nearly everyone is vulnerable to mindless eating. Life is stressful! Feeling stressed out is a common trigger of mindless eating, even for the healthiest of eaters. Linda needed time to relax from her day. She had developed an automatic habit of reaching for food as a way to unwind. On most days, she was more stressed than hungry, judging by the way she grabbed anything. Food can comfort and soothe because it instantly changes your senses and distracts you. Sometimes it is easier to eat mindlessly than to deal directly with the source of stress, particularly if it is something like confronting your boss or apologizing to your spouse.

On the other hand, too much stress can also skew your appetite so that you no longer feel or notice your hunger. Jane didn't eat when she was stressed. When she was a teenager, she had taken care of her alcoholic mother. Jane remembers combing the bars at three o'clock in the morning looking for her mother most nights. As an adult, her life had begun to resemble her mother's misfortunes and mistakes. She got married and then divorced in a very short period. She was moody, lacked energy, had trouble sleeping, didn't enjoy her life, and had zero appetite. She ate barely enough to function. Not eating enough was making her stressed, and being stressed made her not want to eat.

Stress, whether too much or too little, can make it difficult to truly feel your hunger. What's bothering you seems to take center stage.

Skill Builder: *Soothe Stress*

Finding ways to soothe and comfort yourself without food is a big topic. I wrote an entire book about it called *50 Ways to Soothe Yourself without Food*. That book offers ideas for easing stress and tension without eating. Here are two:

- When you feel overwhelmed by stress, sit down in a comfortable place. Curl your toes up tight. Hold for a moment, then release. Next, clench your fists up tight, then release. Press your elbows tight against your sides, then release. Next, squeeze your bottom cheeks together, then release. Move up to your shoulders. Lift your shoulders high up into the air, hold for a moment, and then release. Clench your teeth together and tighten your jaw, and then release. Creating a controlled moment of tension and then removing it can be soothing to your body.

- For another way to release stress, imagine that someone has stuck a paintbrush through the side of your head. The handle is sticking out of the right side and the brush is coming out of the left side. Move your neck up and down as if you are painting with the brush on a canvas. Move just your neck and head. Visualize making large strokes and small ones, or painting a picture. Then imagine the brush coming out of the other side of your head, and repeat.

Skill Builder: *Identify the Issues*

Sadness, frustration, substance abuse, stress, trauma, sexual and emotional abuse, and anxiety are some of the feelings and experiences that can make you particularly vulnerable to mindless eating. Therefore, it is important to identify whether you have any ongoing issues that need to be addressed first to help you get a handle on your eating.

- **Identify the obstacles.** What is clouding your awareness? Depression? Anger? Relationship issues? Reading self-help, medical, and mental health books may be useful. Consult quality websites and experts. Gather and study quality information. See the Resources section at the back of this book for leads.

- **Discuss your problems with a trusted friend.** Talk it out. When you listen to others, you may be surprised by the universality of the human experience of pain and suffering.

- **Consult a professional.** Counseling can help you identify which emotional barriers may be blocking healing
from mindless eating.

#13
"Letting It Go" Mindfully

Make the best use of what is in your power and take the
rest as it happens.

—Epictetus

Victoria had had a tough day at work. All she wanted was a big scoop of strawberry ice cream. While she was licking the sweet, creamy dessert, she didn't think about all the politics happening at work, or any other worries, for that matter. Nothing else was troubling her as long as she was eating.

We hold on tight to positive, happy experiences and avoid negative thoughts and states of mind in the desire to get rid of the negative quickly. *Being mindful* is letting an experience *just be what it is* without trying to change it. *Letting go* is *accepting things the way that they are.* You don't have to like your body or enjoy eating mindfully to be able to accept both your body and the practice of eating mindfully.

Victoria often heard this thought floating through her mind: "I have to get control over my eating habits." Many dieting strategies try to hammer in the concepts of control and willpower. This notion has been detrimental to many, including Victoria.

Food problems are often highly correlated with control issues in general. The desire to be in control may be an attempt to achieve a sense of order and control in life and your body. Choosing to "let go" of the things mostly out of your control is one way to handle the situation. A mindful approach relinquishes efforts to dominate people or events that are utterly out of your control and encourages you to accept change as it happens and take charge of the things that are in your hands. Change is good, natural, and inevitable, even though unfamiliarity produces discomfort. The unease that accompanies change often indicates only that life feels *different*, but it is not necessarily *worse*.

Skill Builder: *Small Ways to Let Go of Control*

Establishing the right mind-set is a beneficial way to begin your practice of letting go. Here are some suggestions:

- **View yourself as being in charge.** Think about being *in charge* as opposed to being *in control* of a task or project, whether that's planning a party or eating dinner. Telling yourself that you are in charge gives you some flexibility and lightens your responsibility. You may not be able to control the outcome, but you can be mindful and engaged in every other way.

- **Refocus.** Is feeling out of control, particularly when you eat, equated to failure in your mind? The next time this happens, reconceptualize this feeling as your go-with-the-flow attitude, or focus on what you learned from the experience.

#14
Letting Go of Dieting

Notice your first reaction after you read the following directive: "Stop dieting." Are you thinking, "I can't let go of dieting! I've been doing it so long!" Or are you saying, "Whew! Finally, I can stop dieting." Your reaction to the instruction to stop dieting tells you how much you've adopted a dieting mind-set. You may need to reprogram your brain to accept that *you* hold the internal wisdom to change the way you eat.

Letting go of dieting can seem unimaginable. If you've been dieting for years it may be difficult to alter your way of thinking. The Buddha taught that cravings and desires keep us stuck and unhappy. To liberate yourself from unhappiness, letting go is necessary. The first step is to look at why dieting has been so important to you. In the case of weight loss, the desire to shed more and more pounds often comes from wanting to look good, to obtain a romantic partner, to be in control, to achieve perfection, or to raise your self-esteem. When you have a specific desire, you begin to cling to it and adopt an "I must have it" attitude: "I want a better body, it's the only way to feel good about myself." But clinging to such a desire causes unhappiness. There is nothing wrong with wanting to be more physically fit. The issue is clinging and being unhappy if you don't get it. Maybe you've even said, "If I lose ten pounds, then I will be happy."

Eating mindfully does not advocate that you eat whatever you want whenever you want. This wouldn't be mindful. Instead, it is achieving balance and equilibrium among the four mindful eating foundations—mindfulness of mind, body, thoughts, and feelings. If you overeat, your body and mind will not be happy. Feeling too full can be as uncomfortable as being too hungry. When you are stuffed with food, your body feels sluggish and/or bloated. It may make you feel guilty. Tricia described overeating as feeling like "an overfilled burrito." She felt that her sides would "spill out," and it was very difficult for her to move her body around when she was too full.

Skill Builder: *Commit to a Mindful Eating Contract*

Adopting a mindful eating approach is a choice and a commitment. It requires a conscious, thoughtful decision. The following contract outlines the basic principles of mindful eating. If you are willing to eat mindfully and are ready to fully reject dieting, you can begin by learning the ins and outs of the basic philosophy that underlies mindful eating.

Start by reading the contract below. Make a written copy of it. As you are writing it, personalize the language to apply to your own struggles. Sign it to acknowledge that you have made an informed and thoughtful decision. Hang up the contract in your kitchen or dining room, or put it where you will see it every day, so you can read it often. As time goes by, you can change or rewrite it as needed.

Mindful Eating Contract

I agree to eat mindfully. I will eat with diligent thought from this point forward.

I agree to change my attitude toward eating completely, on a full-time basis. I understand that diets don't work.

I agree to think about what I eat moment to moment.

I agree to consider each bite on multiple levels by taking into account the taste, texture, quality, bodily reaction, and sensations I experience when I eat.

I agree to eliminate my diet mentality. I will do this by rejecting dieting advice and books, and by becoming nonjudgmental of myself.

I agree to be nonjudgmental of other people's eating habits, weight, and body shape.

I agree to have compassion for myself.

I agree to be mindful of my speech. I will eliminate terms like "restricted" or "forbidden" from my vocabulary, and I will start using words like "healthy," "natural," "organic," and "energizing" both in my thoughts and my conversations.

I agree that being healthy and living mindfully is my number one goal.

I agree to accept myself and my body as they are.

I agree to be aware of the unique eating challenges I face.

I agree to accept how uncomfortable, scary, and wrong it feels to let go of dieting.

Signature: _____

Skill Builder: *Letting Go of Dieting*

Try letting go with a symbolic act. Melanie, for example, wrote a letter to herself describing her unrealistic, destructive dieting schemes and her desire to revamp her body. She took the letter, folded it into the shape of a boat, walked to the lake, put it into the water, and pushed it. She watched it sail away. Later, during the inevitable moments when she was tempted to fall back into mindless dieting, she imagined shoving off her little boat. She remembered her hand pushing it off.

Create your own symbolic act to recall during the moments that challenge your ability to let go of your desire to diet. Throw away your diet books, give away your diet food, put a piece of tape over the numbers on your scale—whatever it takes.

#15
Six Sense Perceptions

Angie was a participant in one of my mindful eating workshops. She told a story about one of her most mindful eating experiences. Last year, she went to a wedding in India. Angie didn't know the language. So when she ordered food, what showed up on her plate was always a bit of a surprise. While it was a challenge, not knowing exactly what she was eating was refreshing. She noticed how complacent she had become about eating. Eating the same peanut butter and jelly sandwich for lunch and pasta for dinner over and over again had made her taste buds dull. She ate those foods in a rote and mindless way. But eating spicy curry, on the other hand, jump-started her taste buds. Not knowing what she was eating forced her to start asking herself questions like "What kind of spice is this—paprika or cumin?" "Do I like it or not?" Stepping out of her normal routine forced her to look at the act of eating with fresh eyes.

Those who practice mindful meditation believe we have six senses, not five. In addition to the obvious five senses (sight, hearing, smell, taste, and touch), mindfulness gurus believe that the most important sensory organ is the mind. Your mind is critical for helping you understand, describe, and interpret what you sense. Your "sixth sense," or mind, is alerted by all your senses tightly woven together, and it interprets what is happening. For this reason, using as many of your senses as possible helps your mind to grasp the whole of an experience.

Skill Builder: *Sensory Meals*

Dine at an ethnic restaurant or prepare a recipe from a culture other than your own. This will show you how to look beyond the obvious and familiar to see what you might not normally notice. If you cook the meal, choose a recipe with exotic spices. Smell them and savor the experience. Cooking a new recipe helps you to break out of your routine. Remember, change is good.

If you choose to dine out, pick a restaurant that will stretch your senses. For example, Ethiopian cooking may encourage you to break out of your typical eating habits. Instead of using utensils, food is scooped up with *injera*, a flat bread shaped rather like a pancake. Using your fingers to carry food to your mouth creates a unique tactile experience unlike any other. Also, in some Asian cultures, it is the norm to loudly slurp soup. Although eating this noisily is taboo in American culture, slurping does add another dimension to experiencing what you are eating.

#16
Using Your Sense of Smell

Imagine for a moment the smell of fresh-baked bread. Now bring to mind the smell of sweet onions and sausage grilling. Paying attention to aromas is a wonderful way to improve mindfulness. Your olfactory system is directly connected to your brain. Unlike other sensations, smells travel directly to your brain and are registered immediately, without having to be interpreted. For that reason, odors can awaken your mind quickly and directly.

For example, when you walk into a library or a doctor's office, you immediately know where you are by the distinct odor alone. The smell can be so familiar that you may be flooded with feelings and memories attached to that smell, such as a kid's fear of visiting the dentist. These smells instantly move you into the moment.

You don't even have to realize that you've perceived a scent for it to have an effect on your mood. For example, a client told me a story about having a strong negative reaction to rose-scented perfume. She'd automatically become irritated when smelling it. Growing up, she had spent a lot of time alone in her room to avoid her family's fighting. Whenever she escaped to her room, she locked the door and opened the window. There was a magnificent rosebush directly underneath her bedroom window, but the wonderful scent could not mask the sound of her parents yelling at each other. And in later years, without her being aware, that scent would trigger her feelings of annoyance. Undoubtedly, aromas shift our mood.

What smells good to you? What food smells turn your stomach? Do you want to eat something just because it smells good, even if it doesn't look good? There are some enticing smells, like the heavily aroma of cookies baking. On the other hand, nothing can make you ill faster than a whiff of spoiled milk.

In a recent study, people were given soup and asked to eat until they were comfortably full (Ramaekers et al. 2011). The researchers pumped out either a low or high level of tomato soup smell while the women in the study ate it. They released the aroma for either 3 or 18 seconds. The researchers found that people ate 9 percent less soup when they smelled it for a longer time and when the aroma was more intense. In theory, smell aids in the enjoyment of the experience of eating, and therefore you are likely to eat less.

Skill Builder: *Wake Up and Smell the Coffee*

Before you eat breakfast in the morning, take a moment to wake up your mind. Think for a moment about the saying, "Wake up and smell the coffee." If you don't drink coffee, you can do the same with herbal tea. Sit down. Place a cup of steaming coffee in a mug. Allow the hot vapors to seep up into your nostrils from a safe distance. Inhale deeply. Just the aroma of coffee is very invigorating. It can help shift your mind into the present moment before you take your first bite of breakfast.

Skill Builder: *Breathe in the Aroma*

Ask yourself, "How much does food impact the way I eat?" Does a pleasant scent lead to impulsively buying a sweet? Or maybe you don't even really think about how your meal smells. Before you take a bite, be sure to take a quick but deep whiff of it. It can take one second or less. Ask yourself, "How does this scent impact the way I am about to take this first bite?"

Skill Builder: *Know Your Nose Meditation*

Wherever you are walking, be mindful of smells. When outside, notice the odors of the air, trees, and plants. Take note of the scents when you enter a room, the fragrances people wear, the odors carried by clothes. Pay special attention to your emotional reactions to food smells. Think about how quickly odors can alter your mood and change what is passing through your mind. Find out which scents elevate your mood and which bring you down. Take a moment to stop and smell the roses, literally.

#17
Minding Your Body

Water and words: easy to pour, impossible to recover.

—Zen proverb

Unfortunately, it is more common for women to be critical of and/ or loathe their bodies than to love them. If you eavesdropped on a group of women at lunch, you would be likely to hear some of them lamenting the fat content of their food or scolding themselves for what they are eating. According to some studies, approximately 80 percent of women in America report being unhappy with their appearance (Costin 1999). Although women still worry more about their bodies, men definitely do too. In fact, the number of men who struggle with body image and healthy eating is growing (Tantleff-Dunn, Barnes, and Larose 2011). It is becoming a more common experience for men to feel bad about their bodies, binge eat, or use unhealthy means to control their weight. Thus, eating struggles can affect you whether you are male or female.

Mindfulness is one way you can deal with negative thoughts about your body. Accepting the present moment, as it is, without judgment is the polar opposite of hateful thoughts about your body.

What most men and women want is for these negative body thoughts to go away. Vanish! But, realistically, these thoughts will pop into your head whether you like it or not. The mindful way to cope is to 1) respond rather than react to these thoughts, and 2) actively work on self-acceptance. A negative reaction to a thought like "I'm so fat" happens when you allow it to spiral into other things you don't like about yourself—"I hate my butt, "No one will ever find me attractive," "I can't stand how I look," et cetera. In other words, you can feed the thoughts like throwing fuel on a flame. Or you can let the thoughts just burn out on their own. When you don't buy in to them with more nit-picking at yourself, sometimes these thoughts lessen and even fade away.

Skill Builder: *Overcoming Negative Body Thoughts*

Stop letting your harsh inner critic get the best of you. Negative thoughts about your body divert your attention away from more important things. When you have "I hate my body" thoughts, practice responding mindfully.

- **Don't judge.** When a negative thought pops into your head, like "I'm so fat," give yourself a gentle nudge and say in a calm and kind way, "There's that negative thought again." The temptation may be to judge the thought by responding, "How could I think something so terrible?" Allow the thought to be what it is without judgment. Say, "It is what it is."

- **Find the source.** Ask yourself, "Where did that thought come from?" Typically, the thought doesn't arrive out of the blue. There is often something else that is bothering you that gets translated into a negative thought about your body. For example, although it seems like quite a stretch, a stressful day at work can evolve into worry about your thighs.

- **Actively let the thought go.** Imagine that negative thought sitting on a cloud, and let that cloud float by you. Your job is to let it go by without trying to reach out, grab the thought, analyze it, wrestle with it, or the like. See it. Let it pass.

- **Channel positive thoughts.** Intentionally place your attention to more affirming thoughts. Notice that they may not be positive thoughts, such as "I like my body." Sometimes this is too great of a stretch. Work on self-acceptance statements like "I accept my body as it is," "My body is healthy," "I appreciate what my body does for me." Focus on neutrality, being nonjudgmental, and, ultimately, compassion toward yourself and your struggles with your body.

Skill Builder: *Reshape Your Eating Culture*

Start to become a more mindful consumer of the media. Be conscious of the kinds of magazines you buy. Are they filled with skinny models who make you unhappy with your body? Tune in to your reaction to ads that push the message that you must be superthin instead of healthy or in the natural body that you have. Surround yourself with more mindful messages. Tear out ads that respect body diversity and hang them on your mirror or refrigerator. There are all kinds of body types—tall, short, thin, curvy, athletic, and so on.

#18
Minding the
"Just Noticeable Difference"

In psychophysics, there is a principle called Weber's Law of the Just Noticeable Difference (JND). Basically, it is the minimum amount by which something must be changed in order to produce a noticeable variation in sensory experience. For example, you would notice if you added 2 pounds to 10 but likely would not if 2 pounds were added to 100. The greater the stimulus, the greater the change necessary to notice a change in it. So you may notice turning up a radio just a little in a quiet room; but it would take a lot to perceive the same volume change at a concert. Marketers often use this principle. They change packaging just barely enough for the consumer to notice it and be interested.

The same thing happens with food. Sometimes it takes a lot of food to make a JND in your stomach. This may be why you keep picking at food. It's unlikely that a bite or two is really perceived. Instead, it takes a large amount to fill up your stomach.

Skill Builder: *How to Stop Grazing and Picking at Food*

Use Weber's Law of JND to help you stop picking and grazing on food. As you pick up your fork or reach for another bite, consider whether picking up this one bit of food will be enough for your stomach to notice it or if you will need to keep eating for it to make any perceivable difference. This is often why people tend to keep eating until they are too full. They continue to pick at food, yet it is not perceived in the stomach.

Determine your average JND. For your stomach to perceive food, how many bites would it take for it to make a just noticeable difference: 2 bites? 20 bites? When you find yourself picking on food, count how many times you take an additional bite. Do you want to take 10 more bites to make it noticeable? Or is it better to skip a bite that won't really be perceived?

Part II

mindfulness of the body

Your body is precious. It is your vehicle for awakening. Treat it with care ... To keep the body in good health is a duty ... otherwise we shall not be able to keep our mind strong and clear.

—Buddha

#19
Meditation: Studying Your Body's Cues Mindfully

In this section, you are going to learn a brief meditation exercise. If you've ever thought, "Meditation is not for me" or "It's too New Age-y," think again. Meditation is just a particular way of tuning in to what is happening in your mind and body. It's not something strange or mystical. This type of introspection is the perfect activity for helping you assess whether you are really hungry or not.

Meditation is a way of stepping inside yourself. It's like taking a flashlight inside your mind to illuminate your inner world. When you meditate, you calm your body and quiet your mind. You start to "hear" the chatter in your mind. In the case of eating, your thoughts play an important role in whether you eat or not. Meditating can help you tune in to these thoughts.

For instance, let's imagine that you suddenly have a food craving. Your mind thinks, "I want chocolate and I have to have it right *now*." An act of meditation could be as simple as turning inward and asking, "Where did that come from?" You may want to locate from where in your body the craving is coming. Is it arising out of a hungry belly? Or is coming from your brain? Maybe the craving is what you *think* you need to take away boredom.

Meditation connects your mind and body so that they form a unified whole. Creating wholeness between your body and mind is extremely important if you are struggling with food issues. In order to recognize the signals your body sends to the brain, the communication between your thoughts and your body needs to flow freely, without obstruction. Your body and mind work together to decide if you are hungry.

Skill Builder: *Reconnecting to Your Body*

Here is an exercise to promote tranquility. It is one of the many meditation techniques for finding soothing, calming inner peace and insight. Use it when you are having difficulty making healthy, mindful food choices, or when you are feeling overwhelmed emotionally. Follow these simple steps:

1. Find a position that allows you to be comfortable but alert. Generally this means sitting or lying down; make sure to allow your body to feel naturally at ease. Take several deep breaths and relax. Don't forget to keep breathing deeply throughout this exercise.

2. Begin by feeling the places on your body that are in contact with other things. For example, feeling the cushion you're sitting on, your feet resting on the floor, your clothes touching your skin. Be aware of your posture. Move slowly through each region of your entire body, and take note of the places where there is tension.

3. Direct your attention to your feet. First tense and then relax the muscles of your feet and toes, and become aware of how they feel.

4. Now direct your awareness to move slowly up your legs, past your knees, to your thighs. First tense and then relax the muscles of your legs and thighs.

5. Tense and then relax your butt and your hips.

6. Tense and then relax your abdominal muscles.

7. Tense and relax your chest and shoulders.

8. Tense and relax the muscles of your arms.

9. Tense and relax your hands and all of your fingers, down to your fingertips.

10. Tense and relax the muscles of your face. Notice the feeling of your tongue inside your mouth, the weight of your eyelids, the heaviness of your neck. Relax your forehead by tensing and letting go. Do the same for your scalp.

If you need assistance, buy a progressive muscle-relaxation recording to walk you through the process of relaxation.

When you have completed this exercise and you are completely relaxed, you will be in touch with what your body feels like at rest. This is valuable information. You can use it to help counter the anxious nervousness that may tempt you to engage in mindless eating.

#20
Releasing Body Tension with Mindful Breathing

Tom learned an important mindfulness skill that involved something he did all the time with no effort whatsoever: breathing. In this section, you will take a brief moment to attend to the way you inhale and exhale. Let's try it right now. Turn your attention to your breathing without trying to change it. Are you breathing fast? Slow? Deep? Shallow? What did you notice? Perhaps you stopped thinking about whatever else that was on your mind and turned your attention only to your chest moving up and down and the air traveling in and out of your nose.

Why is breathing so important, particularly to changing the way you eat? Deep breathing increases the amount of oxygen your brain and bloodstream receive. This leads to clearer thinking and a stronger connection to your body, which helps you to make better decisions about what to eat. Also, when you slow down, you don't just engage in autopilot behavior, you think through your next action. Finally, many people panic a little when they have to make food decisions. This panic creates the fight-or-flight response in our bodies. Calm down a little with a deep breath or two before making a decision about what to eat.

Breathing is the very foundation of living. Keep in mind this great quote by Jon Kabat-Zinn: "Until you stop breathing, there is more right with you than wrong."

Skill Builder: *Take a Breather*

This exercise presents a technique for instantly reconnecting your mind to your body. It is easy to do and immediately starts a calming response. Try doing this several times a day. Use this exercise to take a three-minute mini-vacation from your worries.

1. Find a comfortable posture. Bring your awareness to your body. Pay attention to how all the parts of your body feel.

2. Relax; feel your body getting lighter.

3. Devote your attention to your breathing. Breathe from deep inside your stomach. Put your hands on your stomach and make sure your belly pushes out when you inhale and pulls in when you exhale. This is called "belly breathing." Imagine that you have a balloon inside your stomach. When you breathe in, imagine the balloon expanding and pushing your stomach out.

4. Note the rhythm of your breathing, its coming and going. Pay attention to the feeling of air moving through your nose. Stay aware. Observe.

5. Follow your breathing, don't try to alter it.

6. If you are having difficulty keeping your mind from wandering, count each time you breathe out, one number for each breath. When you reach ten, start over or reverse the count. Feel the difference between counting on the in breaths and the out breaths. Alternatively,

don't count and instead pay attention to the muscles that produce the breath.

7. While you are doing this exercise, in addition to relaxing your body, you are prevented from thinking about anything that might be troubling you during the time you take to do it.

Pay attention to the way you breathe in different situations, such as when you are walking, running, having sex, relieved, happy, sad, or tired.

Skill Builder: *Straws and Bubbles*

If you have difficulty doing the previous breathing exercise, get out a drinking straw. Inhale through your mouth and exhale through the straw. Notice the sensations as you blow out. You can also blow a few breaths quickly through the straw. When you are done with the exercise, you can also use this straw to chew on. Notice whether this alleviates the need to munch on food. Do you find the chewing motion soothing? How long do you feel like chewing?

You can also chew gum. Blow bubbles with the gum. Feel yourself exhale into the gum to make it expand. Listen to it snap as it pops. This can help alter your breathing pattern as well. Notice your breathing as you blow these bubbles.

#21
Moving Your Body Mindfully

Be mindful of how your body moves. Eating is the essential element for making your body *go*. It is like adding gas to your car. In part, how well your body functions and moves depends on your food intake. Are you fueling up? Or are you running on empty? Do you fill up on premium gas—nutritious food—or low-grade junk food? Are you consuming enough protein to power your movements? Or perhaps you are overeating? Maybe you feel the amount you are eating is weighing you down and making it difficult to move.

Investigating what's happening in your body requires conscious thought and your focused attention. Have you ever broken your leg or some other body part? Prior to your accident, it is likely that you didn't really notice how your legs moved, since they were working smoothly. After you break your leg, this suddenly changes. You are likely to become very appreciative of how your legs used to work—carrying you up and down stairs and from one end of the room to the other. The same when you have a cold. You suddenly notice your ability to taste and smell has dissipated. As you recover, you are so glad when everything is working in proper order again. Start to tune in to your body.

Skill Builder: *Be Aware of Moving Mindfully*

Conduct an observational study of your body and its movements. Choose a week and dedicate it to taking note of how your body interacts with the world. Observe your body as if you were watching it in a film, and from the point of view of the main character. You don't have to do anything out of the ordinary, just watch and observe your natural movements.

- **Notice the way you** *eat* **at meals.** Do you take small bites or do you cram your food into your mouth? Do you eat slowly or quickly? Do you eat one food at a time, or do you mix foods together?

- **Notice the way you** *sit.* Do you slump or cross your legs? Do you sit still, or do you shift constantly? Are you relaxed, or does your foot shake? How long can your body sustain sitting in one place?

- **Notice the way you** *move* **while you talk.** Do you use hand gestures? How close do you stand to the person to whom you are speaking? Do you touch others when you talk? Where do you direct your eyes, where do you put your hands, how loud do you talk? What do your non-verbal expressions communicate to others?

- **Notice the way your body can be** *assertive.* Observe how it is actively involved in moving around in the world. Focus on and become aware of your very vigorous, dynamic moments, such as running, throwing, yelling, playing sports, making love.

- **Notice the way your body** *transports* **you.** Appreciate the sensations of walking. Focus on how your legs move, their rhythm, pace, and stride.

- **Notice the way your body** *relaxes.* Focus on how you stretch and move your arms and legs, and how you twist your neck.

- **Notice how you** *lie down.* Do you lie on your stomach, roll over, shift around, or do you stay motionless, not moving at all?

- **Notice the way you** *balance.* Does your body have to work to maintain your balance? Be aware of the occasions when you shift your balance and lean against something.

- **Notice** *internal sensations.* What do your joints and muscles feel when they move? When do they feel sore? When do they feel good?

Skill Builder: *Energizing Food*

Take a moment to tune in to how food makes your body feel. Are you eating foods that invigorate your body? Or are you consuming meals that make you feel so sluggish that you don't want to move? Consider:

1. Do you eat energizing foods? These are foods that provide you with enough vitality and stamina to work, play, and move. If this isn't what you eat, state what kind of

food may give you more energy. For example, adding more protein, committing to eat one fruit a day, et cetera.

2. Do you eat foods that drag down your movements? If so, state one way you may lighten up what you eat. Perhaps it is cutting down on salty food or limiting greasy foods.

Skill Builder: *Meditation Moment*

Imagine putting food into your mouth. Visualize it traveling into your stomach, being converted to energy, and being used by your nerves to send signals to move your body. Think about how one action, like eating, has a ripple effect. Eating well impacts the rest of your body's movements.

#22
Mindful Movement

The foot feels the foot when it feels the ground.

—Buddha

"I have no idea when I am hungry and when I am full." This is a statement made by many of my clients. It's no surprise. Years of yo-yo dieting and mindless overeating interferes with your body's natural, internal signals to put down your fork and pick it up. Is there anything you can do to change this? Yes! Mindful movement can provide an excellent opportunity to reestablish a healthy connection with your body.

Research confirms that it's not just intensive cardio workouts or running that helps people to be more mindful eaters. In fact, the gentle practice of mindful movements and yoga may really be all you need (Framson et al. 2009; McIver, McGartland, and O'Halloran 2009). You may be thinking, "But yoga doesn't make me sweat, how could it help me to manage my weight and appetite?" When you slow down and tune in to yourself, you begin to develop and nurture the important connection between your body and mind that has been destroyed by dieting. Ultimately, yoga helps make you more aware of what you eat and how it feels to be full. When you befriend your body and care for it well through stretching, breathing, and relaxation, you no longer treat it like the enemy. It is only through mindful awareness of your body that you gain more power over your appetite.

Colleagues at the Fred Hutchinson Cancer Research Center in Seattle led a study that found that people who did mindfulness-based yoga could lose pounds and keep from gaining weight during the long term. Participants in the study lost approximately five pounds. Those who were at a healthy weight and practiced yoga for four or more years had a three-pound lower weight gain during the long term than those who didn't do yoga. For people at a higher weight, there was an eighteen-pound difference between those who practiced yoga and those who didn't (Kristal et al. 2005). In a different study, after a twelve-week mindfulness-based yoga treatment program for binge eating, women experienced a healthy reconnection to their body and to food. The women reported they ate more slowly, reduced how much they consumed, chose better foods, and had more positive feelings about their body. Overall, yoga appeared to help the women improve their physical relationship with their body and the way they consumed food (McIver, McGartland, and O'Halloran 2009).

For just a moment, put this book aside and hold one arm up over your head. Keep it there for a minute. Pay attention to what happens in your mind as you do this. Maybe at the beginning your mind is saying, "This is easy" or "I wonder why I am doing this." Toward the end of the minute, perhaps you are thinking, "How much longer?" or "I can't do this anymore." You may notice that your mind became very tuned in to where your arm was positioned in space, the gravity pulling down on your arm, and its movement. Put your arm down. The point of this exercise is that before you raised your arm, it's likely you were not thinking about or "feeling" your arm. Creating tension made you tune in.

Skill Builder: *Mindful-Eating Yoga*

You don't have to become an expert at yoga to reap the benefits of becoming a more mindful eater. Try learning one pose. Visit www.yogajournal.com for an overview of poses, or see the Resources section for more yoga information. Remember that the purpose of this exercise is for you to reconnect with your body, not have an intensive workout. Your aim is to get to know yourself inside and out. Here are some hints to get you started.

- **Adopt a mindful mind-set.** Remember that this activity isn't just about burning calories. It's about developing techniques that tune you in to your body. Yoga helps you to develop mindfulness, good posture and muscle tone, healthful breathing, body confidence, wisdom, patience, discipline, and compassion.

- **Strike a pose.** Try the yoga pose of your choice in a room without mirrors. Looking in mirrors can make you self-conscious. The goal is to tune inward. Doing it perfectly doesn't matter.

- **Use you senses.** Take note of every sensation, no matter how small. This may include how your hair moves against your neck or how your lips part. This is great practice for tuning in to your body when you eat.

- **Accept.** Welcome in whatever feelings come to the surface of your mind when you move. It might be positive thoughts or feelings about the experience, like "This feels good," or negative thoughts, like "This feels uncomfortable."

- **Speak compassionately.** Positive self-talk is part of yoga. While in the pose, say to yourself things like "I feel stronger and more flexible."

- **Push yourself.** You want your body to feel challenged and different. But don't push yourself too hard or you will become frustrated and overwhelmed. You will know when you've reached the challenge point when you start to feel discomfort. This is a challenge you can adapt to eating. Nudge yourself out of your comfort zone by ordering something new or leaving a bite or two on your plate.

- **Allow yourself to stop.** Rest. Again, honoring your body when it is tired or says to stop is critical to becoming a more mindful eater.

Skill Builder: *Mindful Movement*

If you don't have any balance problems, and your doctor okays it, try this exercise. Stand with your feet together. Or if that is too difficult, stand with your feet apart the width of your hips. Put your arms at your side. Inhale as you raise your arms over your head. Turn your palms inward to face each other. Now bend your knees slowly and lower your body as if you are in the process of sitting down onto a chair—though there is not one under you. Exhale as you do this, until your knees are bent at about 45 degrees. Your knees should be behind your toes. Tighten your abdominal muscles. Look forward. Hold for several seconds. Stand up and repeat several times.

You can even practice mindful movement right from your chair. Breathe in deeply. Put your arms to your side. Raise them slowly above your head as if you are guiding the sun high into the sky. Hold for as long as you can.

#23
Acknowledging Consequences Mindfully

The greatest wealth is health.

—Virgil

Heartburn. Gas. Upset stomach. These are some effects that mindless eating can have on your body. Yet your brain works really hard to put that connection out of your mind. You might deny that there is a problem or avoid seeing these issues as side effects of something bigger. You may even chalk up the detrimental effects of mindless eating to other factors in your life, such as stress. Perhaps you may even think to yourself, "Maybe I'll skip on to the next tip because I don't want to think about this." If this is your thought, try to keep your mind focused on this issue for the next few minutes.

Here is what we know: it's tough to keep the balance between eating too much and too little. When you over- or undereat, your body feels uncomfortable, and this discomfort can develop into bigger problems. Your body gives you feedback in the form of physical symptoms. Don't ignore these physical reactions. Learning to see them as useful information can help you to prevent them in the future. Being conscious of the consequences of poor eating habits will naturally lead to more-attentive eating.

People need a base minimum of calories, or fuel, to keep the body from going into starvation mode. (See www.eatright.org to find out specifically how much your body needs to run at its optimal level.) These baseline calories help make your basic bodily functions work: blinking, breathing, sleeping, circulating blood, maintaining a heartbeat. This doesn't include activities like walking, sitting up, thinking, and so forth, which require many more calories. When you lack essential minerals and vitamins, your body struggles to maintain its equilibrium. What's tricky is that you can't see the damage with your eyes. I've seen healthy-looking, thin women walk into my office whose blood work showed a completely different picture.

Overeating is just as problematic. Jessica ignored the health implications of mindless chaotic eating until she got the results of a routine physical. The doctor expressed concern about her high blood pressure and skyrocketing cholesterol. She was pre-diabetic. Jessica was well aware of her labored breathing when she exerted herself physically, but she blamed it on factors other than poor eating habits. After hearing her physician's alarm, it was hard to continue ignoring the warning signs. Jessica finally embraced her health concerns. She came to understand that if she avoided dealing with her health immediately, her problems would worsen.

The key to being more aware of how your body is doing is to use the mindfulness skills of being nonjudgmental, compassionate, and accepting. Avoid judging yourself harshly and just be mindful of the outcome. Note the difference between judging and predicting the physical consequences: "I ate this whole bowl of chips! How could I be so stupid?" versus "If I binge on all of this junk food, the consequence is that my cholesterol will continue to go up, and I will feel bad about doing it." Or "I'm so weak" versus "Eating too much diet food is hard on my body."

Skill Builder: *Mindfulness of Your Body*

Take a step back, observe, and become aware of the sensations within your body. Become acquainted with the *outcome* of mindful and mindless eating. Take out a piece of paper or your laptop and make two columns. Record how your body feels when you eat mindfully and when you eat mindlessly. Try not to *judge*, just *observe*. For example:

Body symptoms: outcome of mindless eating	Body symptoms: outcome of mindful eating
weakness, headaches, gas, chronic tiredness, inability to concentrate, stomach pain	energy, wakefulness, power

#24
Letting Go of Your Former and/or Future Body

Marie kept a picture of herself from high school on the refrigerator. Whenever she glanced at the picture, it upset her. She automatically thought, "I used to be thin and didn't even know it. I also didn't worry about what I ate back them." It's hard to remember that our bodies are constantly changing. We often want to cling to a certain body we've had at a particular moment in time. However, Marie admits remembering that she did not feel happy with herself at the time the photo was taken. Now she wishes she would have appreciated how she looked in that moment in the snapshot.

Longing for the way you looked when you were in high school, college, or before you had a baby can be really upsetting. Grieving over the disappearance of your "former" body can suck away a lot of your emotional energy. Mindfulness embraces change and discourages clinging to the past. Buddha reminded us that "everything changes, nothing remains unchanged."

Dieters spend a lot of time fantasizing about their "future" bodies. For example, Elaine began dieting to lose weight for her wedding. She imagined herself gliding down the aisle in a slimmer body. Three weeks before her wedding, she panicked because she had not made it to her goal weight. She spent more time thinking about how she "should" look in her wedding dress than she did about getting married. Her unhappy thoughts about her weight distracted from the joy of getting married.

The point: Think about your body right now. Appreciate it. Your mind may want to drag you into the past to dwell on how you used to look. Or your thoughts may wish to push you into the future in anticipation of how you may look if you lost weight. Instead, be present with your body right now.

Skill Builder: *Accept Yourself in the Moment*

This exercise is about choosing to accept yourself as you are at this very moment. It emphasizes "letting go" of your desire to change your body radically. Read these affirmations out loud or just bring them to mind when you are making difficult choices about what to eat or whether to feel guilty about what you have eaten.

Mindful Eating Acceptance Affirmations

Mind

I accept that my eating and weight concerns are creating emotional distress, discomfort, and suffering in my life.

I choose to accept my body and weight as they are at this moment.

Committing to accept myself is a choice only I can make.

131

Body

I accept that my genetic inheritance strongly influences my body's shape and weight.

I accept how important it is for me to eat mindfully in order to live a healthy life.

Thoughts

To accept my body and weight does not mean that I am judging them to be perfect.

Acceptance comes from within myself. I don't seek it from the outside.

Feelings

I accept that my worth is not reflected by my weight and shape but, rather, my worth is determined by who I am as a whole person.

Acceptance includes rejecting the cultural and social messages I receive about weight.

#25
Mindfulness of Mirrors

*The wise ones fashioned speech with their thought, sifting
it as grain is sifted through a sieve.*

—Buddha

What's your first reaction to looking in a mirror? Do you think,
"Looking good!"? Or do you peek into the mirror and think,
"Ugh!"? Maybe you wrinkle up your nose and say, "I'm so fat!" as
you look at your reflection. Unfortunately, we often use mirrors
to judge ourselves. They become an evaluative weapon rather
than a tool to simply help you see if your clothes match and if
your hair is in place.

Monica admitted that looking in the mirror was sometimes
tough. She'd pass her reflection in a store window, and her eyes
would instantly go to the part of her body she disliked just to
make sure she still hated it. Mirrors seemed to shine a spotlight
on her thighs. She ignored everything else and focused on the
part she disliked the most—her thighs.

Mindfulness is like looking in a mirror without the commentary. The mirror then reflects only what is presently
occurring, exactly the way it is happening, without bias or distor-
tion. It's your interpretation of what you see that can distort and
twist the image reflected in a mirror.

Skill Builder: *Mindful Mirrors*

Use the mindfulness skill of neutral observation to work on body acceptance and improve your relationship to mirrors.

Stand in front of a mirror. Stay in front of the mirror as long as you can. This can be as short as a few minutes or as long as ten minutes. The point is to continue to observe the way you look beyond your typical comfort level. If you feel an urge to turn away, if you feel silly or are uncomfortable, be mindful of that reaction. Observe the complex interaction of the four foundations of mindfulness, your mind's awareness of how you feel and what you think about your body. Unfortunately, a bad-hair day can draw your attention away from seeing the sparkle in your eyes or the rosy glow of your skin. For this exercise, start with one aspect of your body, such as your hands or neck, and then expand your mindful attention to your entire image. Use all of your observing skills.

Instead of thinking of your reflection as good or bad, be neutral. Use the mindfulness skill of *describing* rather than *judging* your appearance. State, for example, "I have brown, curly hair that reaches my shoulders; it's light with blond streaks." Open your awareness to the smooth texture of your skin and the temperature of the different parts of your body. Feel the roughness of your palms and notice the shades of color in your lips. Instead of judgmental words like "fat," use specific descriptors like "curved," "straight," and "oval" to describe your shape. Draw your attention to the scent of laundry detergent on your clothes and the aroma of your perfume. Notice whether you are tempted to use negative and positive adjectives like "pretty," "ugly," "thin," and "fat." This exercise can help you see yourself as a whole and without judgment.

If your mind starts to wander into the past, thinking or imagining what you used to look like, or if it visualizes the future and how you wish you looked, bring yourself back on track. Close your eyes and begin again. See who you are in the present moment.

#26
Getting Dressed Mindfully

Every day, Julie set her alarm for five o'clock in the morning in order to be at work by eight o'clock. On average, she squandered two hours each morning getting dressed. This seemingly easy task was a daily nightmare. A snug pair of pants or an outfit that made her "feel fat" sent her spiraling into a bad mood for the rest of the day and instigated mindless eating. While getting dressed, she felt ashamed, frustrated, irritated, ugly, and just not good enough. Choosing clothes was even more difficult when she had her period. She mistook normal water retention for weight gain.

Do you spend a long time trying to find an outfit that doesn't make you look fat? Or do you worry a lot about the size on the tag? Maybe you feel great wearing a particular size but upset if you have to wear the next larger one. The lack of size standardization wreaks havoc on people. The same woman can wear a size 10 in one pair of pants and a 12 in another.

A step for Amanda to become more mindful was throwing away her "skinny jeans," the jeans that fit well when she was dieting. She would torture herself by getting them out of the closet and using them to measure how much "fatter" she had become.

The point: clothes can make or break your mood, just like the scale. Give away or throw out any items in your closet that leave you feeling bad about your body. Then concentrate on apparel that pleases you in two categories: fit and feel. Does the dress fit well? Do you like the way a certain fabric feels against your skin? In this way, you use clothing as a tool to help you to be more mindful of your body.

Skill Builder: *Dressing for Emotional Success*

Here are some ideas for becoming a more mindful dresser:

- **Choose comfortable and stylish clothing.** Buy soft, comfy fabrics like cotton and linen, rather than stiff, starchy materials; choose wool pants rather than spandex or tight jeans, short skirts, or hosiery. Wear clothing that feels comfortable. Don't buy anything that is tight on you.

- **Identify one outfit that you look really good in.** Save this outfit to wear on the days when you are highly vulnerable to mindless eating or when you feel uncomfortable in your body.

- **Accept weight fluctuations.** If your clothes feel tight, remember that it may not mean you've gained weight. People experience normal, daily weight fluctuations. Water intake and weather changes can account for slight changes in weight too.

- **Investigate different clothing brands.** Know which designers make clothes that fit your body shape naturally. Stick with those.

- **Choose fit, not size.** Think more about how an article of clothing *fits* rather than its *size*. Remember, no one can see the label but you.

- **Highlight other areas.** Spend more time accentuating other, more-visible parts of your body that you have more control over, such as your hair with a new style, your eyes or lips with makeup, or your neck with jewelry; buy colors that work well with your skin and eyes.

#27
Hunger: Listening to Your Body Mindfully

Sensing whether you are hungry or full is an essential skill for mindful eating. But it is much easier said than done. If you've dieted, it is likely that there have been times when you've ignored your hunger, telling yourself, "Sorry, I know I'm hungry but the diet says, 'No snacks!'" Or the opposite: when eating, your body says, "Stop! I am way too full!" but you keep snacking anyway. Your body may be accustomed to getting mixed messages. Experiencing extremes—being too hungry or too full—on a regular basis can make it difficult to be aware of your true appetite.

Skill Builder: *The Hunger Scale*

When you are about to eat something, ask yourself, "Am I really hungry?" Label your hunger on a scale from 1 to 10: 1 being that you are very hungry, even famished, and 10 being extremely full. If you aren't sure how hungry you are—which is a common feeling among dieters—wait. Delay for a little bit and then ask yourself the same question again. The point is to recognize that there are subtle distinctions between famished and stuffed. You can be a little bit hungry (enough to be satisfied by a snack), content (neither hungry nor full), a little bit full (whereby you still have some room), or completely full (as if you ate a huge holiday meal). Assess your hunger at the beginning of the meal or snack, midway through, and at the end. The Eating Mindfully app can help you track your levels of hunger and fullness.

Skill Builder: *Your Signs of Hunger*

Start listening to your body. Identify the physical cues that tell you when you are hungry—your stomach grumbling or you having low energy. These are more obvious signs. Sometimes, however, the urge to eat can occur more subtly, with confusing signals such as being unable to concentrate or moodiness. The signs are likely to be very specific to you. Therefore, I can give you some hints, but the rest is up to you. The following text offers some guidelines for recognizing the difference between mindful physical hunger and mindless emotional hunger. You may want to add to this list signs that are specific to you.

Mindful Physical Hunger

- Stomach growling

- Low energy

- Hunger grows gradually

- Time has passed since your last meal, and you typically eat at regular intervals

Mindless Emotional Hunger

- Boredom, stress, or anxiety triggers a hungry feeling or the sense that you "need to eat"

- Desire to eat again, after eating recently

- Food isn't satiating you—you can't seem to get enough

- Cravings for certain foods (chocolate, ice cream, etc.) are strong

- Feeling tense, like you need a release

- Desire to eat comes suddenly

Skill Builder: *Am I Hungry?*

It sounds like an easy question. But sometimes it is hard to tell. There are many things that can seem like true hunger but, when put under scrutiny, can appear very different. What prompts you to eat? Sometimes it is not just hunger. Before you take a bite, run through this checklist of possible reasons you may be taking a bite besides satisfying a rumbling stomach. Keep a tally for one day of your common triggers.

_____ The "See It" Effect: Do you want to eat it just because you see it? Eating is sometimes triggered by its mere presence and proximity to you.

_____ French Bakery Effect: Consider how beautiful French pastries are. Do you want it because it is visually appealing? In other words, because it "just looks yummy"?

_____ Cinnamon Roll Effect: Smell is a very powerful determinant of whether you eat something or not. Your perception of pleasurable eating is, in part, based on the aroma. Ask yourself, "Do you want it just because it smells good?"

_____ Emotional Effect: Do you want to enhance or continue a particular emotion by eating. Joy? Happiness? Pleasure?

_____ Dampening Effect: Do you want to tame a particular feeling by eating? Soothe stress? Reduce anxiety? Take away boredom?

_____ Sensation Effect: Sometimes you want a particular taste. Or maybe you desire a creamy texture or cold temperature.

_____ "I Think It" Effect: I think I need it, therefore I do. You may be feeling that you want or need something.

_____ Should Effect: Perhaps a "should" talked you into eating something. You "should" eat an apple.

_____ Mirror Effect: You eat something because someone else is having it—a friend, a colleague, a family member.

_____ Desire Effect: Is it a craving? Cravings often appear suddenly and for something particular.

_____ Procrastination Effect: Sometimes you eat just to avoid doing something you don't want to do, like finish homework or pay bills.

_____ Energy Effect: You may be eating to get a burst of energy.

_____ Routine Effect: Ask yourself whether you are eating now because this is when you always do it.

#28
How Much Do You Weigh Psychologically?

Every morning Becky stripped down, tip-toed onto the scale, and anxiously waited for the results. She weighed herself twice just to reconfirm the number. Sometimes she would weigh herself three times a day. She described herself as a "scale addict." One day Becky decided to go cold turkey and put away her scale for good. After a scale-free month, Becky discovered she was much more in tune with her body. With no numbers to rely on, she had to pay attention to her internal senses. Knowing how her body felt was essential. Overall, she worried less about eating, calories, and numbers. More important, she lowered her anxiety level each morning and gained time for herself during the day.

When you succumb to your scale, you turn over your sense of control to something outside of yourself. When the scale presents you with a number you don't like, you may judge yourself too harshly. This can jeopardize your psychological balance because you become dominated or emotionally weighed down by your self-critical judgments. Rather than judging yourself, it would be more helpful to think about weighing yourself psychologically.

So if you have a love-hate relationship with your scale, I highly recommend that you break up with your scale. Hide it for a while. Tuck it in the back corner of your basement. Stop letting a piece of metal become not only a measure of your weight but the measure of your worth—and a strong determinant of your mood and well-being. Here are ten reasons why you may wish to seriously reconsider your relationship with your scale:

1. If you have ever had a day when you were feeling great and then you stepped on the scale and your day was permanently ruined, then it's time to realize that your scale is taking on the role of an abusive partner. A scale can make or break your mood in an instant. Stop letting the scale play head games with you.

2. If you really want to know how your weight is impacting your health, get a tape measure. What really matters is your waist circumference. According to information from the National Institutes of Health (NIH), large waist circumference is associated with an increased risk of health problems, like type 2 diabetes, dyslipidemia, hypertension, and cardiovascular disease. On average, if you are a male, your waist circumference should be less than 40 inches. If you are a woman, less than 35 inches, according to the NIH.

3. Your weight alone is a poor indicator of your health. You can be very thin and unhealthy (be malnourished or have osteoporosis or high cholesterol, for example) or overweight and healthy (no heart disease, good cholesterol, etc.). Don't get lulled into believing that your weight can determine if you are fit or not. Get a complete physical by your doctor to determine how healthy you are.

4. A scale doesn't tell you about your strength and endurance. Can you run a mile? Can you touch your toes?

Can you walk comfortably? These things are what really matter to your life. Not being able to do these daily activities tells you a lot about the state of your health.

5. Use your clothing as your guide. Your clothes help you to have a better perceptual awareness of your body. Numbers on a scale do not. Your scale may *tell* you that you've lost five pounds—but how do you "know" it? Your clothes help you to sense it. Without even stepping on the scale, clothes alert you to whether you have lost or gained weight.

6. A scale does not measure your body fat–to-muscle ratio. As you become more fit, your muscle mass goes up and therefore your weight increases. A scale is not sophisticated enough to know the difference. Therefore, if you need to know more about your body, get your body fat composition evaluated by a personal trainer at a sports clinic or wellness facility.

7. A scale doesn't consider your healthy weight range. It only gives you one number. Within a day or two, your weight naturally goes up and down depending on things like your water intake, salt consumption, premenstruation, and other factors. It is natural for your weight to fluctuate a little rather than stay on one exact number.

8. A scale cannot measure your self-worth. So if you use your scale for punishment or reinforcement, if you reward yourself when the number is down and penalize yourself when it is up, then stop. A scale should not have that power over you.

9. Not all things can be quantified—though we as human beings love to count things, to see our progress in numbers. Focus on the process of eating mindfully rather than the numbers on a scale. If you are eating healthfully, your weight will drop.

10. Scales are not all the same. Don't be surprised if your weight at home is different than what is recorded at the doctor's office. Scales are machines. While they are relatively on target, for the weight obsessed, even a pound of difference can throw you into an unhealthy tizzy.

For some, a scale is a helpful tool. For others, a scale warps your emotional relationship with your body. If this sounds like you, I hope this has convinced you to rethink your relationship with your scale. Say, "Adiós, scale!"

Skill Builder: *Scaling Back*

If you are unable to separate from your scale or know you will be unable to resist weighing yourself when you find one elsewhere, use mindfulness techniques when weighing yourself. Meditate, breathe, be aware of the process of stepping onto the scale. Follow the feelings and thoughts that arise when you weigh yourself. Don't try to push your feelings away, but embrace them and try to see the influence they have on your mindful or mindless eating. Remember that weight is just the number that says how hard gravity has to work to keep you anchored to Earth. On the moon, you would weigh a lot less. It's just a number. Don't let it keep you down emotionally.

Skill Builder: *Think Health, Not Weight*

Being healthy isn't just about being thin. There are other specific markers of health. A very thin person can be just as unhealthy as someone who is overweight and vice versa. The markers below, taken all together, give a much broader picture of your health than numbers on a scale. Discuss with your physician how your results compare to what is considered normal or healthy for you, and determine if additional tests may be helpful. These markers can open up the discussion beyond weight. The markers below, taken all together, give a much broader picture of your health than numbers on a scale. Ask to have the following checked:

Blood pressure

Resting heart rate

Cholesterol level

Fasting blood glucose level

Triglyceride level

Thyroid levels

C-reactive protein level

BMI (body mass index)

Hip-to-waist ratio

Waist-to-height ratio

Waist circumference

Stress level (high vs. low)

Amount of exercise

Intake of caffeine, alcohol, drugs, medications

Hours of sleep per night

#29
Mindful Cravings

After eating a healthy lunch, Jeff craved something sweet. Ice cream had been on his mind all day, but it wasn't part of his new diet, so he searched the kitchen for something else to eat. After a bowl of cereal, several handfuls of chips, and an apple, he finally ate a bowl of chocolate-chunk ice cream. He had tried to satisfy his food desire with other snacks, but he eventually ate the ice cream anyway. The cereal, chips, and apple added many more calories than he would have consumed if he had eaten the ice cream alone when he became aware of wanting it. A mindful approach would solve this dilemma differently. Jeff would have given himself permission to eat in a mindful way what he really craved instead of trying to ward it off.

Cravings are often the result of deprivation. Typically, you want what you can't have. If you can have it, you won't insist on having it as much. The idea is to give your body just enough of what it wants. Sometimes eating a small square of chocolate can satisfy the desire for sugar as well as an entire candy bar. But if you crave an entire candy bar, eat it joyfully and mindfully. Create balance by eating other healthy foods later.

Mindfulness can help you loosen the grip of cravings. If you experience a sudden urge for pizza, take a deep breath. *Respond* thoughtfully to this craving instead of *reacting* on your first impulse. Get to know the pattern of your cravings. Do you have an urge for something salty and crunchy every afternoon? Do certain environments, like passing a bakery, make you desire a sugar-coated doughnut? By knowing how your cravings work, you can take the power and urgency out of them. You can sometimes anticipate when they will arise and have a plan waiting.

Skill Builder: *Mindfulness of Cravings*

Here are some ways to have a mindful response to cravings:

- **Pinpoint what you usually crave.** If it is chocolate, find a way to satisfy your craving in a mindful way. At work, keep a mini candy bar or a handful of Hershey's Kisses in a drawer to fill that craving. Or carry food with you so you're not tempted. Having a plan makes you less susceptible to feeling out of control. Remember the adage "Whatever you resist, persists." Approach cravings consciously.

- **Respond with the healthiest option possible.** For instance, if you are craving white chocolate, try dark chocolate or chocolate milk, which are healthier and have some positive health benefits, if you think it will satisfy this craving.

- **Do some detective work.** Ask yourself what your cravings suggest about your eating. Are your food desires an indication that you are too restrictive with your food? Do your cravings suggest that you are seeking comfort? Discover what your cravings mean, and find healthy

151

ways to satisfy them. Ask yourself the following questions whenever you find yourself craving a particular food (and see if the sample reply applies to you): *How will satisfying my craving affect my mind?* (I can be more present and focus on what I'm doing if I take care of this craving.) *How will satisfying my craving affect my body?* (It will feel good on my lips.) *How will satisfying my craving affect my mood?* (It will make me feel pleasure and some guilt.) *How will satisfying my craving affect my thoughts about myself?* (I will think that I am someone who takes care of myself.)

#30
Walking or Running
"The Middle Way"

When was the last time you exercised? Was it just yesterday, last week, a long time ago? Mindless eaters often wrestle with maintaining a healthy, moderate amount of exercise and movement in their life. They often fall into two different camps—those who exercise a lot or those who avoid it completely. The goal is to find a middle ground between these two extremes. Buddha notes that extreme tendencies occur when you are having difficulty walking "The Middle Way," or finding your balance between two extremes. Mindful living is a pragmatic, flexible approach to finding what works for you. It is not just about ending unhealthy habits but also about finding other positive, physical activities. Identifying what will work for you realistically is essential to exercising mindfully.

Kristen and Alex are examples of people in these two camps. Kristen knew her exercise habits had grown out of control when she was unable to skip her workout even for one day. It was always her highest priority despite other important events in her life. Exercising dominated her life and schedule.

Alex, on the other hand, always had good intentions to exercise, but she never seemed to have time. When she received her monthly bill from the gym, she hid it under a stack of papers to smother her guilt. She had the same reaction when she examined her body in the mirror. When she saw her protruding stomach and too-tight clothes, she was mortified. Her glances in the mirror lasted only long enough to check that her clothing matched. She posted a photo of herself as a teenager on her refrigerator to motivate herself to lose weight, but the picture only increased her awful feelings about her body. She subconsciously trained her eyes to avoid looking at the photo.

Alex had to be honest and speak compassionately to herself about this problem. The first step was to stop avoiding her bills. Then she had to face her feelings of guilt and just terminate her membership. Gradually, she began doing physical activities that were more compatible with her lifestyle. For example, she had been taking a streetcar and a bus to get to work. Instead, she began walking to the bus rather than riding on the streetcar. That way she got a good walk twice a day. While walking, she focused on her body's movements and all the sensations of walking. It felt good and doable—and it fit into her schedule and didn't cost a dime.

Skill Builder: *Acknowledge Exercise Avoidance*

If, when you hear the word "exercise," you say to yourself, "Ugh!" try thinking about it as "movement." Identify what kind of movement is realistic for your life. Maybe it is walking, running, dancing, or just stretching. Ask yourself right now what kind of movement you *like* to do instead of what you think you *should* do. If you don't know, just start observing what kind of action feels good to you. Is it a brisk walk that creates sweat or just an easy walk to loosen up your muscles?

Start small and work your way up. Focus on achievable exercise, or movement, goals. Once you reach your first goal, bump it up only slightly. "Slightly" is the key word. Increase your exercise only after you've fully mastered your first goal. The most common mistake is to expect too much at once. Failing at an unrealistic, unachievable goal will cripple your motivation. Setting and reaching goals is the best way to maintain an exercise regimen and gain a sense of accomplishment.

Adding more movement in your daily routine is a natural, easy way to increase exercise. Small, mindful changes, like parking at the far end of the parking lot so you will be forced to walk farther, taking the stairs instead of the elevator, stretching hourly at your desk, or taking a baby for a walk in a stroller, can make a big difference in the long run.

If you become bored, distracted, or unhappy with your movements, be aware of the feelings that arise when you think about exercise. Acknowledging these feelings can help you to identify what you need to change about your exercise routines. If you are bored, add some excitement by taking a salsa class or exercising to a workout DVD. If high-impact exercise like running makes you too tired, try a low-impact exercise like stretching.

Finally, know that not all exercise is healthy. Doing it excessively can turn a healthy behavior into a harmful one. Do a movement study on yourself. This self-study will focus on discovering your workout pattern. What prompts you to work out? Is it a feeling? A routine? To be healthy? For muscle development? What function does working out serve? If your body says, "Stop!" do you ignore the warning? Your body sends your mind vital information for making decisions, and you should heed any cues that signal a problem, such as pain, overexertion, or obsession. Athletes are particularly vulnerable to overworking their bodies. Many believe that weight loss enhances performance. Although it may slightly maximize performance, that advantage will not last if you are not consuming an adequate amount of food. Food fosters power, strength, and mental concentration. Consult a professional about your concerns to maximize your health and enhance your athletic performance.

#31
Should You Clean Your Plate?

Wouldn't it be nice to eat like a kid again? We can learn many mindful lessons from the way small kids eat. If you've cared for small children, you know that healthy babies generally don't overeat. Babies cry to alert others when they need to be fed. Infants cannot be forced to nurse or to finish a bottle when they have had enough. This suggests that we are born with biological sensors that dictate how much we should eat, and that overeating is, in part, a learned behavior. In other words, we start out with the instinctive ability to eat mindfully and, somewhere along the way, this changes. Wouldn't it be nice to redevelop those natural instincts?

One way overeating and undereating may be learned is at the family dinner table. Although parents are much more mindful these days about the harm they can do in forcing their kids to eat, it's tough when you don't want to waste any food or you have made a special meal. Many of my clients talk about being a member of the Clean Plate Club growing up. Their parents sometimes forced them to finish all the food on their plates. Or they applied guilt by saying things like "Kids in Africa would love to have those peas." This push to finish rather than listening to the body's fullness cue sets up a lifelong pattern of estimating how much to eat by how much is set in front of you instead of by when the body is satisfied.

If you always eat what is put in front of you, you are likely to be in trouble. Restaurant portions are out of control and

157

completely out of sync with mindful eating. Supersized, gargantuan portions encourage mindless eating.

Susan's first step to becoming a more mindful eater was to interrupt old habits. This included being more mindful of how much she ordered and ate at restaurants. She went out to dinner with her husband several nights a week. Instead of consuming everything on her plate, she noticed that she felt full after eating about two-thirds of the portion. She knew this was her logical stopping point. But just saying stop wasn't enough—she also had the waiter quickly take it away. This interrupted the habit. If she didn't have the plate removed from the table, she would continue to pick at the remaining food. Susan noticed that when she did eat everything on her plate, she became too full, which was the signal that she had not eaten mindfully.

Skill Builder: *Mindfully Clean Your Plate*

Learn some ways to have a mindful relationship with the food on your plate:

- **Experiment with portion sizes.** Try eating different amounts of different foods until you discover what amount seems to leave you feeling neither too full nor too hungry.

- **Don't finish your meal.** If you struggle with breaking the habit of cleaning your plate, leave some food, even if it is just one bite.

- **Take lessons from being a kid.** Use your fingers. Play with your food. Have a small snack during the day to help regulate your hunger.

- **Examine how you finish a meal.** Consider for a moment whether you use internal or external cues to signal when you're done eating. External cues are things like the waiter takes away your plate, the lunch hour is over, the bag of popcorn is empty. Internal cues are things like you feel full, you think about the portion size, you feel thirsty. Listen to internal cues to know when to stop.

#32
Fine-Tuning Your Palate

"I just love food." This statement is often made by overeaters to explain why mindless eating happens. On the surface, it seems to make perfect sense. Yet we have to be careful about this way of thinking. Mindful eaters, I would argue, enjoy food too. It's not a lack of pleasure in food that cultivates eating healthy portion sizes. So is overeating really about loving food? Or is it about loving the feeling that food produces? I'd argue more for the latter.

What would you say if I asked you to pick your favorite French fry from a restaurant? It could be from a fast-food restaurant or from a fine-dining establishment. Or choose another type of food you crave. Pick only one establishment as your favorite. Stop for a moment here and make your selection. Now think about why you chose those particular fries as your favorite.

Next, let's think about how you chose your favorite and what this exercise brings to mind. First, this shows that French fries are not all the same. There are differences in texture and taste. Some are crispier, saltier, soggier, thinner, thicker, longer, shorter, et cetera. It's likely that you considered these factors, whether consciously or unconsciously, in making your selection. Perhaps you said to yourself something like "I like X place best because their fries are always just salty and crispy enough but not too salty."

Fine-tuning your palate by asking yourself these kinds of questions is a task that all over- and undereaters must undertake.

People who overeat may not be discriminating enough about their tastes. Undereaters need to get back in touch with the pleasurable aspects of food. This may have fallen by the wayside if you are avoiding treats or eating only diet foods. Remember that it's okay to eat things that taste good but are not healthy. But really define and narrow down your choices to what you like the very best. If you love vanilla cake, turn your nose up at all types that aren't your absolute favorite. Maybe you are afraid that eating your favorite is likely to spur a craving for more instead of less. The more you fine-tune your taste buds, the better. By knowing your taste buds well, you will have a much better idea how to satisfy the craving. This skill also helps you to narrow down your food choices and to eliminate foods that are only mediocre to you.

Skill Builder: *Apple Experiment*

Practice fine-tuning your palate. Buy six different varieties of apples. There are many different kinds, and they range in color from yellow to red to green to pinkish. In addition to diverse colors, they vary from sweet to tart, as well as in crispness. In other words, an apple isn't just an apple.

Place six paper plates in front of you. Cut one slice out of each apple and write on the bottom of the plate which type it is. Mix up the order of the plates so you don't know which variety is on each plate.

Take a bite. Describe it to yourself. On the paper plate, write some descriptors: crispy, sweet, dry, juicy, et cetera. You may notice that you have to compare this bite with another bite to even be truly aware of the taste. You have just fine-tuned your apple taste buds and discovered that apple varieties taste different from one another. What did you learn about your own taste buds? Did you prefer sweet or tart? Did your sense of smell help you to differentiate among them?

Part III

mindfulness of feelings

By effort and heedfulness, discipline and self-mastery, let the wise one make for himself an island, which no flood can overwhelm.

—Buddha

#33
Mindfully Coping with Emotional Eating

Feelings are like the weather, natural yet uncontrollable. Similar to clouds sweeping over a sunny day, emotions change quickly. Unfortunately, you can't control the weather or your feelings. The best you can do is to forecast the conditions and prepare for them—take along an umbrella or a rain jacket. The same can be said for emotional eating. When you get to know your feelings well, you can predict your mood. Then you can arm yourself with the tools you need to cope with those feelings without food or any kind of mindless eating.

Strong emotions also cloud your awareness, making it difficult to make objective decisions about what to eat. In the heat of an angry moment, you may say, "I don't care if I eat junk food" or "What the heck, I'll eat it anyway," when really you do mind. Sometimes people make feelings worse by how they react and label them. Instead of just noticing how you feel, you may find yourself categorizing your emotions in the same way you would everyday things—into three simple categories: pleasant, unpleasant, or neutral. Labeling a feeling as unpleasant can intensify it. For example, if you say, "This day was lousy," your body is listening. It will respond with the body movements to convey that you've had a crummy day. Your mind might answer, "Crummy day equals stress eating."

Skill Builder: *Finding the Emotional Trigger*

Meditation brings wisdom; lack of meditation leaves ignorance. Know well what leads you forward and what holds you back, and choose the path that leads to wisdom.

—Buddha

If you have an episode of mindless eating, contemplate what events happened *right before* it. Start at the incidence and mentally walk through the experience backward. You will be looking for an emotional trigger. It may be stress, loneliness, anger, et cetera. Examining the context of the situation leads you back to the feelings and thoughts that prompted the situation. There are many factors that could have made you susceptible to uncontrolled eating.

Where were you?

What were you doing?

What were you feeling?

What's tricky is when the emotional trigger didn't happen immediately before the mindless eating. Let's say that yesterday your boyfriend said something insensitive. You put it aside. Then it began to fester in your mind overnight, and then the next day something briefly flashed across your mind and you suddenly felt vulnerable. So the trigger can happen earlier in the day, the day before, or the previous week.

After you walk through the incident backward, walk through it again going forward this time. Be aware of the feelings that occurred after your bout of mindless eating.

Once you have identified each behavior that led to the incident, try to identify the points when you might have taken a divergent path. Was there a fork in the road where you could have taken a different direction? For example, maybe you could have done your homework in your bedroom instead of the kitchen to prevent mindlessly picking at food when you got bored with studying. Commit the circumstances of this critical juncture to your memory.

#34
Enduring Difficult Moods

Have you ever felt that one minute you're on top of the world and the next you're in a deep, dark hole that you can't get out of? Let's face it: emotions can take you on a roller-coaster ride. Whether good or bad, intense emotions become overwhelming and often intolerable. In general, the wish is to *get rid of them* as soon as possible. Eating is one way to change or adjust your emotions quickly. It can do many things. People eat food to stuff down feelings, or they starve themselves and thus ward off feeling anything at all. Munching on food soothes, diminishes, distracts, and/or can intensify feelings. Eating and/or not eating can also be a vehicle for releasing emotions, and to regain control over moods.

Skill Builder: *Melting Feelings*

Remember, feelings come and go and evolve quickly, which demands a watchful and flexible eye. Think about something that really upset you in the past. Today, it is more than likely that the event doesn't bother you at all. You might even laugh about it. Just because you feel an emotion doesn't mean you have to do anything about it. Remember, they are just feelings, not permanent facts.

If there is a feeling (like guilt or regret over what you ate) that is bothering you, get out an ice cube. Sit down and hold the ice cube in your hand. Notice what is happening in your mind as you hold it. At first, you might experience pain. Your mind might say, "This is awful" or "This is too cold, I can't stand this." Stick with it if you can. Keep the feeling you are struggling with in mind. The ice cube will begin to melt. Continue to hold it until it is just a puddle of water. This exercise demonstrates how your feelings can melt too. Your emotions will transform and melt away if you continue to stick with them and wait patiently until they dissipate, despite the initial discomfort.

Skill Builder: *Don't Let Your Emotions Eat You Up*

These exercises will help you cope with difficult emotions in the moment rather than allowing them to consume you.

- **Identify the feeling.** Full awareness is always the key. Write a letter to yourself describing the emotion. Observe it first, then describe it.

- **Bump it down a notch.** Imagine that you can quantify the level of your emotion and adjust it, just as you can tune the dial that sets your speaker volume. If you are at ten, make a plan about what needs to happen to reduce it to a six.

- **Let your body go.** If you are feeling anxious, reconnect with your body. Feel your feet against the floor. Let your shoulders and neck drop. Observe how it feels not to resist the pull of gravity.

- **Take a virtual massage.** If you are feeling stressed, imagine giving yourself a body massage. Picture yourself lying on your stomach. Imagine being massaged with scented oil. In your mind, start at the top of your head. Allow the massage to travel down your neck, shoulders, arms, and fingers. Finish up by imagining your calves and ankles and finally your feet.

- **If you feel sad, be sad.** Don't fight it. Rent a sad movie, call a friend, and talk about it. Teach yourself that bad feelings aren't intolerable or scary. They can be accepted.

- **Take a good look at anger.** Anger is a particularly difficult emotion. It often occurs secondary to a primary emotion. Frustration, hurt, or fear of loss may be behind an angry feeling. Admit your anger and discover what is prompting it. Take a mental snapshot of the moment. Step back and take the same picture with a panoramic lens. What else is in the picture? Buddha said, "Holding on to anger is like grasping a hot coal with the intent of throwing it at someone else; but you are the one who gets burned."

- **Welcome guilt.** If you're feeling guilty, welcome in that feeling. Remember that mindfulness is about being non-judgmental. If you see yourself sentencing yourself to a punishment, think again. Handing out a punishment will only start another mindless eating cycle. You gain more power by being compassionate with yourself, and your compassion will prevent negative feelings from arising that could trigger more mindless eating.

- **Release pressure.** If you are feeling overwhelmed by emotions and, typically, you push them down, imagine you have a pressure valve somewhere on your body. Turn the knob slowly. Let out a little bit of emotion at a time. Remember, you are in charge of turning the handle.

- **Have daily rituals.** Observing midday and/or end-of-the-day rituals can be a helpful way to release emotions that build up. Daily routines have a grounding effect and foster awareness. Write one page in your journal, sing a soothing song, burn incense, or repeat a prayer aloud. Try to do this at the same time every day. Practicing a ritual is similar to the feelings you get when you hear a song you know well. It is familiar, uncomplicated, and you can predict how much you will like it.

- **Get help.** If you feel as if you want to harm yourself, call 911. When you want to injure yourself, this means that the emotions you are experiencing are too intense for you to contain. Find a safe place with people who can help you moderate and understand your feelings.

#35
Mindful Metaphors:
Visualizing Your Feelings

*I am terrified of eating and getting fat, because I fear
blowing up like a big, red beach ball. The kind of ball that
people kick around and let float away when they don't feel
like it's worth rescuing out of deep water.*

*I felt like I was in an eating coma. I suddenly woke up and
realized how much I ate!*

*I feel skinless. Any kind of emotion feels like it is touching
my raw nerve endings. When people look at me, I feel
naked and unprotected.*

These statements are metaphors that my clients created to
describe the experience of mindless eating. A metaphor is simply
transforming your experience into an image or a story. This
image can help you take a step back so you can observe your feelings from an entirely different perspective. Many of my clients
say they feel like they are in a trance when eating a food they
crave. This description tells me, and them, a lot about what they
are feeling. It puts new words to feeling out of control and numb.

Here is another example. When Kate struggled to eat
enough good, nutritious food, she created a metaphor to describe
this. She compared her body's chronic fatigue and sluggishness
to a car sputtering to a stop because it's out of gas. She visualized
herself as a little blue Volvo, and the food she ate as putting fuel

in the tank. The busier she was, and the harder she pushed down on the pedal, the more often she had to fill the tank with quality gas (protein, complex carbohydrates), not the cheap gas (diet sodas, cookies, chips). Kate became more mindful of the way her body moved and of its many critical functions like breathing and walking. She realized that if she was not mindful, she would be driving down a road that would crash and ruin her body.

Skill Builder: *Creating Mindful Eating Metaphors*

Create your own metaphor. If this is difficult, imagine watching yourself eating on a movie screen. Would you compare the way you eat to an animal, person, place, activity, or object? Once you have this image, you can begin to transform it into a more mindful picture. So if you see yourself hunting down food like a lion, begin to *transform* the metaphor. Notice I didn't say *change* it. Instead, it may be watching the lion walking peacefully away from the hunt. Consciously bring this picture to mind.

#36
Taking a Mindful Breath

If you don't know how you feel, your breathing will tell you. Breathing reflects your emotions. If you are anxious, it is shallow and fast; if you are relaxed, it is slow and rhythmic. When you hold your breath, that is a strong clue that you might be frightened or anxious. When in love, your breath is "taken away." Therefore, by paying attention to your breathing, you can become aware of your inner emotions. If you don't know what you are feeling, stop, pay attention to your breathing, and let your breathing help you tune in to your feelings.

Skill Builder: *Deep Breathing Before You Eat*

For many people, eating is a stressful event. If this is so for you, sit down at the table and prepare yourself to be in a mindful state before you eat.

Focus all of your attention on your bodily sensations. Relax and make yourself comfortable. Lean back in your chair and be aware of the position of your body. Relax your muscles, close your eyes, and let your body unwind. Tense and release your muscles. Begin by taking a deep breath. Very slowly, take a deep breath that allows your diaphragm to move up and down. Concentrate on the sound of your breath. Listen to it and feel the sensations as you breathe. Feel yourself relax as the tension releases and leaves your body. Follow the journey of the air as it travels through your nose and throat, fills up your lungs, and moves your chest. Take just a moment to connect with your breathing as you gear up to eat mindfully.

#37
Mindful Eating and Relationships

Andrea noticed something very unusual about the way she ate. When she went out to dinner with Hannah, she ate mindfully and ordered just an entrée, which filled her up. Dinner dates with Julie, however, did not follow that pattern. They started with drinks and appetizers and then progressed to a meal and dessert. She left feeling stuffed. Meeting up with Helen was an entirely different experience. Andrea ordered only salad, because that's what Helen always ordered.

Who you eat with matters. It can help or hurt your efforts to eat mindfully. In fact, a study in the *American Journal of Medicine* found that a person's chances of becoming obese increase by 57 percent if he or she has a friend who is obese (Christakis and Fowler 2007). Among spouses, the likelihood that the other spouse would become obese increased by 37 percent. Be mindful of whom you dine with and how they impact the way you snack and eat meals.

Skill Builder: *Minding Your Friends*

You don't have to drop friends who eat too much, or seek out new companions who eat mindfully. Instead, just begin to be more mindful of the impact they have on you. Notice whether you order similar dishes. Pay attention to how fast they eat. Do you eat at the exact same rate? Unconsciously mimicking a friend's eating behavior can lead you right into mindless eating.

Try this experiment. When you are eating with someone, try to match his pace. When he takes a bite, you take a bite. Notice how this feels to you. Does it seem fast? Slow? Then do the opposite. When he takes a bite and chews, you wait. The point of this exercise is to be conscious of the fact that how someone eats may or may not match your natural tendencies. Be wary of unconsciously following his habits.

#38
Heart versus Hunger Cravings

Your work is to discover your world and then with all your heart give yourself to it.

—Buddha

Buddhist theory identifies cravings as the root of suffering. Emotional cravings can be more powerful, insatiable, and destructive than cravings for ice cream or chocolate. Your emotional desires aren't as clear-cut or as predictable as your desire to eat. As you become more mindful, you will begin to realize exactly what your heart hungers for. Examples include cravings for companionship, love, power, and control. In contrast to food, these longings are not as easily fulfilled. Sometimes people misinterpret their heart cravings and try to feed their bodies when they actually need to take better care of their souls.

For example, two feelings derailed Jessica's diet. When she was lonely or sad, all she could think about was comfort foods like biscuits and gravy and pecan pie. Food had been her companion when she felt miserable. Yet the goodness of the dense pie and fluffy biscuits was fleeting. When she stopped eating, the loneliness came right back, sometimes even worse. Now, instead of reaching for food as comfort, she mindfully calls a friend, sends an e-mail, or engages in social networking. It feels so good to connect with others that she stops thinking about overeating and rejoices in companionship.

Skill Builder: *Keep a Mindfulness Journal*

Keep track of your constantly changing emotions and desires. Carry a small pocket journal with you wherever you go. Make it easily accessible so you can reach it in the moment you experience fleeting, powerful, or intense emotions or cravings. Or buy a daily calendar that breaks down the day by hour. Or use an app on your phone. Jot down the emotions you felt at particular hours. Examine the calendar at the end of the day to see whether any patterns or trends emerge. If you spend most of your time in front of a computer, create an easily accessible, secure document file to record what happens to you emotionally when your mind wanders during the day. Whenever your mind says, "Gotta have _____ [chocolate, junk food, etc.]" pause for a moment and immediately write down how you are feeling.

In addition to your feelings, record and examine your daydreams. These can give you a good idea of what you are consciously craving. If you imagine a special relationship, you are likely craving love and attention. If you dream about a job promotion, you may be longing for power, control, and intellectual stimulation. Consider what you can do to satisfy your heart's cravings.

#39
Mindful Holiday Feasting

Do you look forward to traditional holiday feasts with dread or delight? If you said dread, you aren't alone. The stretch between fall and the beginning of the new year are often times of celebration for everyone—except for mindless eaters. Buffets, holiday cookies, and traditional family foods you get only once a year are extremely challenging. Gatherings centered exclusively around food can turn not-so-merry. Worry about gaining extra holiday pounds is nothing to celebrate. Holidays often elevate feasting to a special status, and they encourage mindless eating by inviting all to overeat.

Spending time with relatives during holidays is another surefire way to trigger mindless eating. Reconnecting with family can be as stressful as it is joyous. You might find that you get very emotional. Conflict is more likely to erupt. Hanging out with your family can reignite feelings of inadequacy or of being controlled or rejected, or of wanting to please. Or it may bring up intense memories of happy holidays from the past, which can make you miss more-regular contact with your family.

Skill Builder: *Approaching Holiday Meals Mindfully*

To help prevent falling into the trap of mindless eating during large, festive meals, refer to these tips often:

- **Plan ahead.** One mindful approach is to offer to help prepare meals. This will give you greater control over the menu.

- **Time it wisely.** Advocate for keeping the meal at a regular mealtime. Too often, we schedule holiday meals in the afternoon, which interrupts people's regular hunger schedule.

- **Don't overbake.** Be sensible with food gifts. Stop giving three dozen cookies. Instead, give just a few. If you receive several dozen cookies, give some away.

- **Snack slowly.** When you snack on holiday foods, be sure to sit down. Savor. Take mindful bites. It's a perfect time to really enjoy what you are eating—mindfully.

- **Snack early.** If the holiday meal is to be eaten at someone else's home, eat a snack before you go. Don't wait until after the football game or holiday parade. If you do, your body will send you hunger cues that may be difficult to satisfy in a mindful manner.

- **Celebrate what's significant.** Connect yourself with the meaning of the holiday. For example, if it is the Fourth of July, celebrate the liberty you have to choose your foods.

- **Stay present.** To prevent overeating, stay in touch with the experience on a moment-to-moment basis. At the table, eat slowly and look at everything. Smell and taste your food. Breathe in the holiday atmosphere.

- **Pause between servings.** After finishing your plate, wait twenty minutes before getting a second helping. It takes the part of your brain that helps to regulate your appetite about twenty minutes to register what you ate and to send the information that you are full to your body and brain. Allow your body and mind the necessary time to send and receive these signals.

- **Be discriminating.** If the same food is prepared in different ways, choose your favorite. For example, if there are mashed potatoes and sweet potatoes, consider which will give you the most pleasure, or have a small amount of both.

- **Be aware of portion size.** If you usually have trouble knowing how much you have eaten, put the food on your plate in piles that don't overlap. Start with this, and then wait and see how your body responds.

#40
Dining Out Mindfully

Jill loves interesting, quaint cafés and was a regular at many local Thai restaurants. She disliked cooking, and the flavors she found at restaurants far surpassed anything she could create. The dark side of eating out, though, was worrying about excess calories. She had no control over how the food was prepared, and because she didn't know how many calories she was consuming, she felt guilty. Still, when she dined out as a reward to herself, she mindlessly overate. Eating at restaurants was equal parts pleasure and remorse.

The good news is that you don't have to stop eating at restaurants if you are trying to manage your weight. A study in the *Journal of Nutrition Education and Behavior* found that women who frequently ate at restaurants actually lost weight after they learned mindful eating skills. They reduced their intake by approximately 300 calories even though they weren't "dieting" (Timmerman and Brown 2012). Although the mindfulness skills were geared toward eating better at restaurants, the researchers found that women also used the mindful eating skills at home. In other words, mindful eating skills help you to improve your dining habits whether you are eating at your kitchen table or at a five-star restaurant.

Many restaurant-goers think, "Eating out is special and a treat, and therefore I should eat whatever I want." But it doesn't have to be that way. If you eat out a lot too, the good news is that you can use mindfulness skills as you would at home. Attentive, aware, nonjudgmental eating can take place anywhere. Learn to think of the restaurant's ambience and service, and the fact that you don't have to clean up, as the real treat.

Skill Builder: *How to Dine Out Mindfully*

Going to a restaurant can lead to all sorts of mindless eating behaviors. But it doesn't have to be that way if you follow some of these tips:

- **Choose wisely.** The first step in planning an evening out is to choose a restaurant mindfully. This means picking one with a large selection of healthy, interesting foods. Avoid buffet-style, all-you-can-eat, fixed-price, or three-course meals, or places with limited selections. This approach is similar to avoiding the grocery store when you are hungry. Make a plan in advance: look at menus online. Try to choose a full-service restaurant over fast-food and a local rather than chain restaurant—it's easier for chefs to change the entrees to your liking if they aren't premade.

- **Eat an apple.** According to one study, eating an apple before your lunch can decrease how much you eat at lunch by 15 percent (Flood-Obbagy and Rolls 2009). The fiber in the apple, or any piece of fruit, helps fill you up, potentially helping you to avoid overeating. But also, tasting a sweet, crunchy piece of fruit can move you into a mindful state of mind.

- **Order soup.** Consuming soup before the main entree reduced consumption of the meal by 20 percent, according to one study (Flood-Obbagy and Rolls 2007). The water in the soup helps fill you up. Also, eating soup is a process that is done slowly. This can also help to move you into a mindful mind-set before you eat your meal.

- **Order a salad.** Consuming a large, low-calorie salad (with small amounts of cheese and dressing) before a meal makes you feel more satisfied and decreases consumption during the meal by approximately 12 percent (Rolls, Roe, and Meengs 2004).

- **Drink water.** Drink at least sixteen ounces of water. Water is an effective way to help you manage your weight and appetite (Dennis et al. 2010).

- **Drink mindfully.** Ordering alcohol with your meal can increase mindless eating. Also, be aware that drinks have nutrients (or lack them) and calories.

- **Eat your favorite food last.** Save your favorite food until the end of the meal. A study in the journal *Appetite* found that people who had a cookie after a meal rather than before it tended to remember eating it more after time had passed (Robinson and Higgs 2011). Thus, keeping the experience fresh in your mind will make it less likely that you will reach for another cookie or treat later.

- **Don't go out *really* hungry.** When you are moderately hungry as opposed to very hungry, it is much easier to make mindful choices and to refuse food you normally wouldn't eat. Very hungry people are likely to eat anything put in front of them. Moderately hungry people are choosier.

- **Choose good dining companions.** Eat with people who are good, mindful eating role models as much as possible.

- **Share an appetizer or a dessert.** Ask someone at your table to split an order with you. Discuss your likes and dislikes rather than dwelling on food that you "can't have." Have fun.

- **Don't judge what others eat.** No one wants to dine with someone who criticizes his food choices. If someone chooses greasy French fries that you wouldn't dare touch, be aware of your reaction. Say to yourself, "I'm judging, and I need to be more compassionate. I notice that I become envious and critical at the same time. I need to focus on my eating and my eating alone." At other times, you might feel guilty that your "thinner" companion is eating less than you are. Again, be mindful of your needs and everything going on within yourself.

- **Minimize celebratory outings.** Try to curtail going to a restaurant as a way to celebrate or provide pleasure—even if the meal is for someone else. Buy her a gift, send a card, leave a very thoughtful voice mail message instead of going out to dinner. Until you have a better handle on eating mindfully, dining out on special occasions can be very challenging, since it reinforces the notion that food provides the ultimate comfort, which it doesn't. If your friends ask you out to dinner frequently, suggest meeting for coffee or tea instead. Plan nonfood-related activities like going for a walk or to the movies. Or invite your friends to a dinner that you will prepare.

- **Avoid picking at your food.** When bread is brought to your table, take a piece or two, and send the rest away. Bread (and butter) are among the most common mindlessly eaten foods. When you are done with your meal, move your plate to the side, or ask to have it removed. It's easy to put more food on your plate mindlessly—or to pick at what's left—when it is in front of you.

- **Minimize business lunches and dinners.** Try not to conduct business meetings or important discussions over a meal. It is difficult to be attentive to your eating when you must engage in critical or emotional conversation at the table. People tend to use food unconsciously to soothe tension, too, so schedule meetings without food (or with only healthy foods) when possible.

#41
Accepting Your Genes

Ella's family joked that she, like other women in the family, had been cursed with the "Cervelloni hips." The women on her father's side all had wide, sturdy hips and buttocks that were a painful contrast to the thin, elegant hips and dainty butt that she fantasized about when she worked out. When she examined her family lineage in old photos, it was clear that her desire to fit into a much smaller size petite pants was unrealistic. No matter how much she dieted and worked out, her bone structure and her body type would not change. Body shape and weight range are largely influenced by genetics. Your bone size, metabolism rate, and fat deposit locations are determined by your genetic code as much as your eye color, hair color, and height are written into your genes.

Accepting your body is key to eating more mindfully. This is sometimes confusing. You may mistake the message of acceptance to be one of defeat that nothing can change. This isn't it at all. Too often we fight our natural shape with dieting and try to mold our bodies into an unrealistic shape. By accepting your body, you can feed it according to how your body *is*, not how you *want* it to be. When you start doing this, your actions change.

The "set point" theory postulates that your body has a genetically predetermined weight range. Your body tries to keep your weight within that range and will automatically adjust your metabolism and food-storage capacity to keep you from losing or gaining weight outside of that range, or set point.

In addition, the set point theory posits that the environment helps to determine if your body settles at the top or the bottom of your natural weight range. Thus, if you are dating someone who is an extremely healthy eater, it may be more likely that your weight will be at the lower end of your natural weight range. In contrast, if you are dating someone who loves junk food, you may find your weight rising to the top of the range.

April, for example, was five feet, three inches tall. Her weight fell naturally within a range of plus or minus 10 pounds. If she ate mindfully, her body weight stayed comfortably within this range. She noticed that it was extremely difficult to lose any weight at the bottom of her range, and her body felt uncomfortable when it broached the upper limit. April's ability to listen to her body helped her to eat mindfully and to stay within her natural range.

Skill Builder: *Identify Your Natural Body Shape*

Draw a family tree. Identify those family members who have struggled with mindless eating. If food and weight haven't been a topic of conversation, look at family pictures. Take into account how bodies changed from childhood to old age. Think about whether over-, under-, or chaotic eating is a family pattern. While you are at it, appreciate the family traits that people admire and compliment, like unique green eyes or naturally curly hair.

Role Models

Besides your primary caregivers, there were many other people who impacted the way you ate growing up. Pause for a moment and bring these people to mind. Perhaps you ate lunch at school with your best friend. You ate what she ate.

If you were adopted or frequently ate with people other than your biological parents, your primary caregivers still played a significant role in shaping your eating habits. They did this by what they fed you and the messages about food they taught to you. Tracy's adoptive mother provides a poignant example of how subtle, mindless eating habits are learned. Although Tracy's mother did not encourage her daughter to diet, she was constantly trying out the latest fad diet. Her mother never ate the elaborate meals she prepared for her family. Tracy observed her mother's eating habits and subconsciously incorporated them into her own routines. She wouldn't eat foods her mom avoided because they had "too much fat." Never underestimate the importance of your environment and role models.

Skill Builder: *Identify Learned Food Habits*

Be mindful of the "typical meal" you ate while growing up. Sit still for a moment and bring to mind a typical family meal as a child. Visualize it. Did you sit at a kitchen table or eat off of TV trays in front of the television? Maybe you ate alone or cooked your own meals. Perhaps you had to share food with your siblings and you never could seem to get enough. What feelings pop up as you think about this image? Welcome in this image, even if it is a painful one.

Now do some reflective writing.

1. List how many times a day you ate when you were a child (maybe you skipped breakfast or snacked many times a day).

2. What did you typically eat at meals and for snacks?

3. What messages did you receive about your body, about food, and about how to eat?

4. Did these messages change as an adolescent?

5. How do those messages affect you now?

6. What kind of food culture do you want to create in your own family, dorm, or household?

#42
Changing Mindless Eating Traps

Debbie's desk drawer was filled with candy—caramels, chocolate, gummy bears, and the like. Whenever she sat down at her desk, she automatically opened the drawer and searched for her favorite candy. This routine happened virtually every single day.

Mindless eating is likely to occur in the same place, over and over again. To make life simpler, the mind takes advantage of any shortcuts it can. For example, when you are looking for underwear, your hand will automatically go to your underwear drawer. If you rearrange your drawers and put your underwear in a new location, your hand will still tend to travel automatically to the old drawer, until new shortcuts are formed in your brain. We make connections between events, and we have to work hard to break and form new links.

If you practice mindless eating in certain places, your brain is likely to subconsciously remember that and act out of habit. What are your hot spots for mindless eating? One might be in your car; maybe you wait until you are alone and swing through the drive-thru. Or perhaps it is when you are lying on your bed at night watching TV. Or sitting in front of your desk.

Jessica's vulnerable spot was in her kitchen. To take control, Jessica created a mindful eating haven in her home. This was away from the refrigerator, phone, TV, and other distractions. Before eating, she put all the food portions she planned to eat on the table, so she would not have to return to the kitchen. She learned to relax and breathe between each bite, and to watch herself in the process of eating. This slowed her down enough to enjoy her meals in a mindful way.

Skill Builder: *Pinpoint Your Mindless Eating Cues*

Identify the *places* you are most likely to eat mindlessly: in the kitchen, at the local coffee shop, at your desk? Find ways to turn a space in your environment into a place that fosters mindful eating. Remove any clutter that could distract you while you eat. Objects like phones or clocks that pull you away from a mindful state should be moved elsewhere.

Or create a new space. Tailor it to be a calm, peaceful environment that brings you to a mindful state. If you wish, burn incense or change the lighting. Add a pretty tablecloth and fresh flowers. Play soothing music. Hang up a sign in your danger area that reads "Eat Mindfully" to re-alert you to your mindful stance.

Put your place setting so that it faces away from the kitchen (or refrigerator). Bring food to the table before you eat, so you won't have to get up.

#43
Filling Up on Fun

"I'm so bored!" Unfortunately, boredom and a feeling of emptiness are very common reasons that people eat when they are not hungry. Eating, or continuously thinking about eating, fills up a stretch of time and can feel purposeful. The emptiness of being alone can be as painful as a hollow stomach. If thinking about eating takes over a significant amount of your day, you may want to consider reorganizing your energy. Be mindful of other activities that will satisfy you as much as food does—and that will feed your soul, as well.

Skill Builder: *Boredom Blockers*

Make a list of activities that will keep you from reaching for food or thinking about food during downtimes. As the Buddha said, "A generous heart, kind speech, and compassionate service to others are renewing forces." Be actively aware, awake, and moving. Mindfully go shopping, read, participate in hobbies and sports, call someone, take a nap. Write in your journal. Turn your thoughts to being mindful of others. By far, the best way to fill your heart and mind is to spend time with caring friends. Whatever you choose to do, feed your mind by participating actively in the world.

Skill Builder: *Ho-Hum Meditation*

You can't keep yourself entertained 24/7. Sometimes you will be bored. Part of the challenge is to be okay with a still and quiet mind. Set a timer for three minutes. Find a pleasant place to sit. You can close your eyes or not. Do what feels comfortable. Your job is to empty out your mind as if you are emptying out your laundry bin. Just sit with the stillness. If this is difficult, focus on one object. If your mind wanders or you try to entertain yourself with thoughts, bring your focus back to this object. Don't *do* anything until the timer goes off. Notice what happens in your mind. At first, your thoughts may be "I can't take this" or "This is so boring." That is okay and actually the point. Your goal is to get to the point where you can tolerate boredom without having to fill it up with food.

#44
The Mindful Mirror

It was Jackie's night to dine out with her girlfriends. Jackie sat among her five friends at the restaurant in front of wall-to-wall mirrors. They ordered a bowl of chips and *queso* for the women at the table to share.

As soon as she started eating, Jackie dug into the bowl, thrilled by how wonderful the melted, spicy cheese tasted. While she was eating and talking, she causally caught sight of herself in the mirror. She watched herself intently and was surprised by what she saw. It was like watching someone else. Her hands moved mechanically, dipping the chips in the *queso* methodically in a steady rhythm rather than as if she was aware of and taking joy in what she was eating. This sight moved her out of autopilot.

This is much like listening to yourself on the answering machine or seeing yourself in a video. Watching or hearing ourselves from a distance gives us a different perspective.

Skill Builder: *Mindful Mirror*

For one meal, sit in front of the mirror. Remember that this exercise is not to judge yourself. You may notice your mind wanting to critique how you eat. Or you might feel a little self-conscious.

Simply notice whether judgmental thoughts come up and inter-fere with how you are eating. You may notice how quickly you eat. Or you may become more aware of your hands and how they pick up food—small forkfuls or large, heaping ones. Simply watch.

Part IV

mindfulness of thoughts

The thought manifests as the word; the word manifests as the deed; the deed develops into habit; and habit hardens into character. So watch the thought and its ways with care, and let it spring from love born out of concern for all beings.

—Buddha

#45
Mindful and Mindless Contemplation

How does mindlessness impact your decision making? There are three sneaky ways that your brain tends to lapse into mindless thinking. They are very subtle, so unless you are aware of how they impact your thinking, they can rule the way you eat. Why is this important? Thoughts precede your behavior. So it's crucial to tweak your thoughts before you actually try to change your behavior. To learn more about how to change your thinking, see my book *But I Deserve This Chocolate! The 50 Most Common Diet-Derailing Excuses and How to Outwit Them.*

1. **Pigeon-Hole Thinking:** In the absence of more info, your mind tends to just default to stereotypes. For example, instead of thinking through whether peanut butter would be good for you since it has a lot of protein, you default to the stereotype that it has a lot of fat, and you avoid it. The benefit of simply using stereotypes is that it makes all of your choices much easier. Let's face it, you make hundreds of decisions every day about what to eat and what not to eat. This can be exhausting! The downside is that you aren't thinking through the facts or making considered choices.

2. **Robotic Thinking:** The mind is often mentally over-loaded and needs a break. Perhaps you've said that you

are in an "eating trance" or an "eating coma," or that you've zoned out while eating. It is a state of not thinking or not paying attention while having a meal. The problem with robotic thinking is that you don't think through whether something—or its size—is a satisfactory choice. When you don't feel or think anything, you don't tune in to your stomach or mind.

3. **Automatic or Routine Thinking:** This is classic autopilot behavior. The good news is that acting on autopilot or out of habit can make life very easy and simple. Routine can be helpful—but it can be at the root cause of mindless eating. For example, lapsing into the same snacks or eating habitually at night during your favorite TV show is mindless behavior.

Skill Builder: *Change Mindless Thinking*

For one week, keep track of the thinking traps you fall into. Just observe. Then, for another week, try out these suggestions:

- A mindful remedy for pigeon-hole thinking: Listen closely to your thoughts. Notice whether you use any self-imposed rules or blanket statements to decide what to eat. Such statements may start out with "I always eat that …" or "The rule is …" Instead of automatically following the rule, think it through. Say to yourself, "That's a snap judgments. My choice is …"

- A mindful remedy for robotic thinking: Allow yourself some time to de-stress, unwind, and relax. Get out of the kitchen. Lie down. Put your feet up for a few minutes. Find other mindless activities to help give your mind a break. Flip through TV channels or a magazine. Knit. Doodle. Surf the Net. Check e-mails. Peruse social networking sites.

- A mindful remedy for routine thinking: Throughout the day, recognize when you are shifting into a routine—for example, drinking coffee every morning or leaving the house at the same time. Shake up your ordinary routines. Eat after you walk the dog instead of before. Change the place where you eat. You can also make healthy eating your default habit. Perhaps you eat fruit as a snack every day.

#46
Changing Mindless Thinking

As the fletcher whittles and makes straight his arrows, so the master directs his straying thoughts.

—Buddha

People who struggle with their eating often have distorted thinking patterns that are similar to the distortions of fun-house mirrors. You might think something like, "I totally blew it," when you've just had a couple bites of something sweet. Or "I'm so stuffed, I feel like I've gained five pounds," even though it is impossible to gain weight that quickly. These thoughts aren't true reflections of reality. Regardless, the way you think impacts how you eat.

Mindless thinking is automatic. These thoughts jump into your mind without any effort whatsoever even though you know they aren't rational. The thoughts play like background music in your mind. Most of the thoughts are extreme—black or white. When you are mindful, you look at your thoughts from The Middle Way—a stance in between the two extreme ends of the spectrum. If you don't notice mindless thinking, it continues. It's like getting your car stuck in the mud. The more your wheels spin, the deeper the car will sink.

Thinking in The Middle Way brings temperate, moderate thoughts that are in the moment, observant, nonjudgmental, and accepting.

Here are nine types of mindless thinking—and how The Middle Way would deal with the issues.

1. **Extreme Thinking:** This type of thinking is dominated by "either/or" thoughts. People who practice extreme thinking don't allow any room for a middle ground or gray area. *Examples:* "I am either perfect or I am a failure," "I am either beautiful or I am ugly." The Middle Way would say, "I may not be happy with every aspect of my body. There are many things I like about my body and myself. There are some things I do not."

2. **Worst-Case Scenario:** This is the mental habit of overgeneralizing the potential outcome of a situation. *Example:* "If I eat this cookie, I will gain ten pounds, and no one will ever want to go out with me again." The Middle Way would say, "I will not gain ten pounds if I eat this cookie. I am trying to eat moderately to feel better about myself. People like me for many other reasons besides my body."

3. **Overstating the Facts:** This consists of sweeping statements that use one rule and apply it to a number of situations. *Example:* "Being fat means you must be lazy." The Middle Way would say, "Being overweight does not imply anything about a person's energy or personality. That is a judgmental, mindless thought."

4. **Turning the Micro into Macro:** This mental habit blows up the importance of an issue to gargantuan proportions. *Example:* "If I overeat again, my life will be ruined forever." The Middle Way would say, "I don't like

it when I overeat. It is very hard on my body, and I feel bad after I do it."

5. **Abracadabra Thoughts:** These consist of superstitious beliefs that seem to hold special powers. *Example:* "If I run three miles a day, I will not gain weight." The Middle Way would say, "How much weight I lose depends on many different factors. I want to exercise to be healthy."

6. **Putting on the Blinders:** This takes place when you ignore important information. *Example:* "I don't see any evidence of physical problems, so my doctor must be wrong. The way I eat is not harmful to me." The Middle Way would say, "I know mindless eating is not good for my body. Although I was uncomfortable when my doctor pointed this out, I realize the impact unhealthy eating can have over the long run, and I am aware of the consequences."

7. **Overdoing It:** These are thoughts that inflate one's importance or relevance to a situation. *Example:* "Everyone is looking at my body. They are all laughing at me." The Middle Way would say, "I am exaggerating. I am feeling quite vulnerable right now. A glance is just a glance."

8. **Random Theories:** These are personal theories developed from faulty thoughts. *Example:* "If I exercise to get rid of calories, I will feel relieved. So if I continue to exercise, I will never feel distressed again." The Middle Way would say, "There are lots of things besides extreme exercise that help me feel relaxed. It's not the only way."

9. **No Backup:** These are assumptions that are made without any concrete evidence to support them. *Example:* "People always like those who are thin and exercise a lot." The Middle Way would say, "I would like this to be true because it would help me feel more in control. However, I know I don't like everyone who is thin and exercises a lot. So this must not be true."

Skill Builder: *Observing and Healing Mindless Thoughts*

Identify which types of mindless thinking frequently pop into your mind. When you catch yourself thinking in any of these ways, say to yourself, "That is an example of 'extreme thinking' [or _____], and it is affecting what I decide to eat." Then ask yourself, "If I followed The Middle Way, how would that thought be phrased?"

#47
Impartial Thoughts

Good. Bad. Right. Wrong. These are just a few of the labels you might attach to the way you eat. Obviously, negative labels can be harmful. Telling yourself that you were bad for eating a sweet can make you feel like a bad person. However, positive phrases like "I'm eating right" or "I am a good person for resisting potato chips" can also be detrimental. Any words with either pleasant or critical connotations distract from just being mindful of the experience. Positive and negative words have a lot of power to reinforce or punish you. When you give yourself a pat on the back, you have to be cautious not to use that same hand to beat yourself down when you make a mistake.

Resisting a handful of potato chips may be an example either of mindful or mindless eating depending on a variety of factors, such as how hungry you are or whether eating the potato chips is in the context of a binge. The same item of food may be considered "good" at one time and "bad" at another.

Eating that isn't evaluated as good or bad is considered "neutral." Neutral experiences tend to slip out of your awareness. Fruits and vegetables are often neutral foods. Typically, eating an apple produces few to no emotions. If you are eating an apple mindfully, you are more likely to think about its juiciness, crunchiness, and tartness than your feelings. Such "neutral" experiences of eating show that it is possible to eat without a lot of emotion

Consider for a moment the last time you felt content after a meal—notice that I didn't say happy or unhappy but simply okay with the outcome. This is a radically different way, for many of us, to think about the outcome of a meal. We often judge it to be a good or bad meal and check off whether it fulfilled what we were looking for, whether it brought a particular feeling— pleasure, fullness, joy.

This can lead to mindless eating. You continue to eat because you want that particular feeling. And if you don't get it, you might keep eating and eating. In many ways it is helpful to orient your mind to focus on a feeling you don't often notice— which is contentment.

Contentment is a good example of mindfulness because it is neutral and accepts things as they are even if it's not what you want. It is just "okay." Unfortunately, we are generally not raised to feel just contented. In fact, it's often quite the contrary. We are taught to want more, look for something better, keep desiring, and continue striving to be happy. Being content is unfortunately pretty undervalued, but it is key to mindful eating.

Skill Builder: *Think about Food Impartially*

Practice this exercise after a meal or snack. When you hear your mind saying, "Just one more bite" or "More, please" or "I want to feel full," find a word or term of contentment to repeat, such as: agreeable, appeased, at ease, acceptable, okay, can't complain, comfortable, complacent, contented, fulfilled, gratified, pleased, peaceful, peace of mind, satisfied, or comforting. Imagine these words passing by you as if on a ticker tape. Keep these words ever present in your mind.

#48
Mindful Imagery

He is able who thinks he is able.

—Buddha

Mark couldn't imagine that he could eat more mindfully. This may have been his very problem. If you don't feel ready to make a change, or if you feel stuck, imagery may be exactly what you need to get you going. Imagining a successful outcome is essential to changing any kind of behavior. Likewise, if you fixate on the reasoning that "using my imagination won't change my eating," no change is what's likely to happen as a result. So do the opposite. Imagine a positive outcome and it can get you there.

According to the psychological principle of "self-fulfilling prophecies," your behavior unconsciously leads you right down the path toward what you are expecting. If you expect to fail, you will unknowingly act in ways that make failure more likely. The opposite is equally true. If you expect to succeed, then imagery can help you to do actions you never thought you could, like eating a piece of fruit instead of a sweet.

Using imagery, you can step back from the experience and imagine a healthy, desirable outcome. This skill values the power of thinking positive thoughts.

Skill Building: *Using Guided Imagery*

When you have a few peaceful moments, close your eyes and walk through these scenarios from start to finish. Imagine these eating situations in great detail. Visualize what you are wearing, the color of the walls, what the food looks like, how it smells, et cetera. State exactly what you will say. This imagery practice can help to raise your confidence. It will make it easier to do it in person if you've "seen" yourself do it already.

Scenarios

- Saying no to a food pusher

- Ignoring a critical thought about your body

- Choosing just the right amount of food

- Avoiding an impulse buy; putting it back

- Eating a reasonable portion of a food you love

- Going to the grocery store and sticking to the list

- Eating at a restaurant and making a good choice

- Going through a fast-food drive-thru without buying anything

- Being bored and finding something to do besides eating

- Feeling stressed and finding something to eat

- Having a craving

- Add your own: _____

Here is a detailed example of guided imagery:

Breathe slowly and deeply in and out. Close your eyes and continue to breathe from your diaphragm. Imagine walking into your favorite Italian restaurant. As you enter, you begin to pick up the mouthwatering odors of garlic and spices. Breathe them in and out. Focus on your breathing and your senses. Relax. Look around the restaurant. Imagine sitting down at a table. The tablecloth is a checkered red-and-white pattern. There is a long, red candle stuck in an empty wine bottle. It is lit. Watch the flame flicker. In the background, you hear soft Italian music. Focus on how you're feeling. Be in touch with all of your senses.

The waiter comes to your table and hands you a menu. As you open it, check out your feelings. What are they? Name them to yourself. Your eyes scan the menu for something that entices you. What thoughts come to mind? Label them as just thoughts. What feelings flow in and out of your consciousness? Do you feel overwhelmed by the choices or guilty for desiring a certain food? Focus on your feelings and your breathing.

Now imagine the food you want to eat arriving at your table. Examine the dish you ordered. Describe its smell, texture, and taste. How does it feel in your mouth, against your tongue, teeth, and lips, as it travels to your stomach? Imagine eating this meal with all your mindful skills in place: being observant, accepting, nonjudgmental, and aware of any lingering thoughts of failure. How does it feel within your body? Stay with every emotion that comes up for you. Name those emotions.

#49
Mindful Realism

Believe nothing, no matter where you read it, or who said it, no matter if I have said it, unless it agrees with your own reason and your own common sense.

—Buddha

Stacy struggled with overeating for more than ten years. She frequently snacked on junk food. Typically she ate out of boredom and loneliness. Regardless of numerous diets and attempts at therapy, once she began eating, she felt unable to leave the kitchen. One day, while she was eating everything she could get her hands on, her dog, Mickey, her long-time companion, sat at her feet and looked up at her. According to Stacy, the look in Mickey's eyes indicated that he cared about what she was doing. At that point, Stacy put down the food, left the kitchen, and took Mickey for a walk. During the walk, she focused and meditated on the sense of peacefulness she felt. Thereafter, whenever she had the urge to binge, she took Mickey for a walk around the block. You won't find any documented "Walk Your Dog" methods to control your eating in any diet books. Nevertheless, walking the dog worked for Stacy.

A mindful mind-set encourages you to eat what works well in your life, rather than what you *think* is right or correct. Mindfulness doesn't strive for a particular result or require a specific change, the way we often arbitrarily pick a number to be a weight goal. In fact, it doesn't dictate anything you should or should not do, because that boils down to making a judgment. Thus, be suspicious of diets professing to be the "only way" to lose weight. There are many strategies for improving your eating habits. Food myths and fad diets all profess to know what is "right" to eat but, unfortunately, they all contradict each other.

The nice thing about mindful eating is that you can apply it to any kind of eating style that works for you. Mindful eating can be applied to those who are vegetarians, who have a special diet due to an allergy like gluten, or who eat a particular ethnic food.

In a nutshell, any strategy that helps you to eat mindfully, provided that it is nutritious and realistic, can be employed. When people choose diets and foods they don't like, or that aren't compatible with their lifestyle, those diets and foods simply won't work. The key is knowing yourself well. This will help you to identify what is doable, safe, and pragmatic.

The overall message is to focus less on goals and critical "shoulds" and "shouldn'ts" and more on an awareness of what works.

Skill Builder: *Your Personal Food Myths*

Make a list of your food myths. These are the behaviors that you believe you "should" be doing. For example, one food myth is that all sweets are "bad" and should be strictly avoided. After listing your myths about "right" and "wrong" foods, transform these into mindful attitudes that are realistic and likely to work.

A more flexible stance in this example might be that eating too many sweets is unhealthy, but eating an occasional, moderately portioned dessert is realistic, pragmatic, and doable.

It is important to consult a registered dietitian about the food myths you've accepted. When you have become entangled in mindless eating, it may be hard to know whether your nutritional knowledge is on target or skewed. A woman in counseling admitted feeling very guilty after eating a bowlful of carrots. She defined this as overeating. Although carrots are healthy vegetables, a bowlful of anything seemed wrong. Her mind had lost the ability to observe her behavior in a realistic manner.

#50
Thinking Out Mindful Meals

Full concentration is essential to being mindful. One very common hindrance to straightforward, peaceful, mindful eating is inconsistency in your eating patterns. It's tough to fully engage in work or play when you are extremely hungry. You may notice that you can't think about anything else but food. Nor can you be fully present after you've overeaten. Your thoughts become very distracted by your discomfort.

Vicky fell into the habit of skipping breakfast and then overeating at lunch. Skimping on her calorie intake in the morning made her ravenous at midday. She often overate at lunch because she believed she had room to "make up" for the calories she had missed at breakfast. Vicky ended up eating more calories than she would have if she had had a sensible breakfast and been only moderately hungry at lunch.

Perhaps your fear is that if you eat regularly or follow a structured meal plan you will cause weight gain. However, as regular eating patterns develop, weight tends to stabilize or drop due to newly consistent patterns of mindful eating. Structure a meal plan that includes three meals a day and two snacks with no more than three-hour gaps between. Make it feasible, realistic, and easy for your schedule. Incorporate as many mindful meals as possible into your daily life.

Skill Builder: *Mindful Meal Planning*

With some prudent planning and conscientious thinking, you can devise mindful meals for the week ahead.

- **Eat a minimum of three times a day.** Eat breakfast and have small snacks. This is as important as putting gas in your car. Without fuel, your car isn't going to move, and neither will you. If you feel the urge to put something in your mouth and you really aren't hungry, drink cold water. Sip the water slowly. Drink sparkling mineral water to feel the bubbles tickling your tongue. Buy flavored or vitamin-enriched water.

- **Eat every three hours.** Eat something small every three hours or so in accordance with your hunger. This prevents the urge to binge.

- **Follow a balanced meal plan.** If you follow a special diet that is vegetarian or gluten free, for example, you may need to be particularly attentive to balance. No matter what, make sure you obtain a well-rounded, sufficient amount of protein, vitamins, and minerals. Pay attention to your body's cues and the signals it may send requesting more iron, calcium, or other vitamins and minerals.

- **Get your energy from food.** If you rely on coffee, tea, or caffeinated drinks to get you through the day, it's important to bring this to your awareness. Pay attention to your energy levels. Think about whether you are using caffeine as a food substitute. Make it a goal to get enough energy via your food.

- **Check your vitamin intake.** Although everyone needs vitamins, it is best to get your vitamins from the original food source. The food primes your body to use the vitamins in the best possible way. When you salivate in response to food, it's an indication that your brain knows what is coming and sends signals throughout your body. Your brain doesn't react in the same way to vitamin pills. Eating whole foods is more mindful than taking vitamins because your entire body is integrated in the experience.

- **Plan your meals for the day.** Having food accessible and convenient will prevent you from grabbing whatever is sitting around.

- **Choose hot foods.** When you are really hungry, eat something hot. Hot foods are often more filling and stimulate more internal sensation than cold foods.

- **Avoid finger foods or appetizers.** It's easier to overeat or binge on these foods because they skew your perception of portion size.

- **Steer clear of binge foods.** If you have trouble with binges, don't buy foods that are likely to make you binge or overeat, at least at first. Make your home and workspace totally free of your favorite binge foods. Once you become more mindful and in better control of your eating, the presence of tempting foods shouldn't be a problem. However, at the beginning, make it as easy for yourself as possible. If you have the urge to binge and the food is present, *leave the room* for at least ten minutes.

- **Consult a registered dietitian.** To obtain information about the basic food groups (protein, dairy, fruits and vegetables, grains), speak with an expert. This will help you understand what would be a healthy food plan for you. Get accurate information. Don't rely on what you read in trendy magazines.

- **Avoid drugs and alcohol.** These increase your vulnerability to eating mindlessly. Alcohol provides an abundance of mindless calories, and it reduces your ability to describe and observe your body sensations. Both alcohol and drugs compromise the precision, clarity, and purity of sensation that is necessary for mindful eating.

#51
Hearing Your Inner Food Critic

Sarah had an eating "oops." She ate two desserts instead of one at a special anniversary dinner even though she had promised herself that she wouldn't. She already felt guilty because she had vowed not to drown her frustration in chocolate after a dreaded visit from her mother-in-law but she had done it anyway. Now Sarah had a choice. She could either calmly and compassionately talk herself through the incident, or she could let her inner critic go to town ruminating, feeling guilty, and criticizing her for the misstep.

Your inner critic can be pretty punitive and unforgiving. Think for a moment about some of the names your inner critic has called you: weak, stupid, fat, and so on. These thoughts can be like a sportscaster's comments during the final seconds of a game. Instead of just observing what is happening, sportscasters describe mistakes in a disparaging manner. Their tone is distinct, critical, and judgmental. They announce how the "right" play "should" have been executed. Similarly, your inner food critic may give you a play-by-play commentary about what you "should" or "should not" be eating.

Judgmental remarks are damaging for many reasons, but mainly because thinking such thoughts pulls your senses away from fully experiencing eating. Who can enjoy food when your mind keeps chanting, "You appall me! How can you eat that!"? These thoughts make you feel bad about yourself, which often leads to more mindless eating—not less.

219

It might sound easy to get rid of hypercritical judgments. However, you may notice that it is harder than you think. The mind clings to this way of speech to try to control and limit mindless eating. The inner food critic is a master at inducing shame, self-hate, guilt, and regret in the hopes of getting you to eat more mindfully. Ironically, these feelings are the prime instigators rather than stoppers of mindless eating.

Compassion is key to helping you manage your weight and change your thinking. It seems counterintuitive if you've been indoctrinated with a diet mentality that suggests that you are a failure if you don't have perfect control over your body and cravings. It would be nice if an eating oops didn't throw you into such a tailspin. Guilt and bad feelings often lead to comfort eating and self-sabotage.

Compassion sometimes doesn't come naturally. Our minds are trained to home in on mistakes and errors. It can be like a mental scavenger hunt actively looking for what you do "wrong" instead of what you do "right." So if you overeat and are tempted to berate yourself, think again. Remember that being critical of yourself does *not* inspire you to change. Think of how empowering a kind word from a parent or spouse is and how damaging a critical statement can be. A harsh word can play in your mind on repeat for years. An easy way to start being more compassionate is to give a stranger a genuine compliment. Kindness is like a boomerang. It returns to you.

Skill Builder: *Silencing the Inner Food Critic with Compassion*

Praise and blame, gain and loss, pleasure and sorrow come and go like the wind. To be happy, rest like a giant tree, in the midst of them all

—Buddha

Sit still and turn your mind inward. Center yourself. Think about a recent incident of mindless eating. When your inner food critic speaks, what does it say? Notice *how* it talks to you. Is it yelling, whispering, nudging, urging, or sarcastic? Allow the thoughts to arise, and just take note of them. Try not to judge yourself for the thoughts but simply acknowledge the content and tone of your inner speech. Are these words like a punching bag in your gut? Do they sting your self-esteem? Do harsh words make you lose your appetite and the ability to taste and enjoy the food that sustains you?

Respond instead of *react* to your inner critic. You may notice yourself arguing with your internal nemesis. Perhaps you respond with "I'm not stupid for eating that!" or "I *do* have control over myself." Instead of getting into an emotional struggle, say, "Okay, I welcome in this thought. I don't have to believe the thought or act as if it is true."

Practice using the compassionate Buddha voice within you to counter your inner sportscaster. Choose an empathetic and kind quote to be your mantra. When you have an eating uh-oh, repeat the mantra silently to yourself many times a day.

#52
Enhancing Your Eating Memory

Why do you mindlessly continue to eat after you've had enough? In part, it is simply because you forget how much you eat. If only your mind were like a computer—simply add another chip to increase your memory capacity. It's likely that you have a lot to remember in your life. So it makes sense that you can genuinely and innocently forget about a snack you had in the afternoon. Therefore, if you are going to eat mindfully, you have to improve your memory capacity a little bit.

In one study, participants who watched TV while eating lunch ate more than subjects who did not watch TV. In addition, people who watched TV during lunch ate more food later during the day (Higgs and Woodward 2009). The researchers hypothesized that the subjects ate more during lunch because the experience was less satisfying. However, they also suspected that watching TV interfered with encoding the experience into their memory. Basically, the researchers concluded that the subjects ate more because the experience didn't get transferred to their memory; researches have concluded that memory plays an important role in appetite control (Higgs and Donohoe 2011). The takeaway: Focus on your meal instead of disconnecting mentally.

Skill Builder: *Enhance Your Meal Memory*

These tips can help you to remember what you ate:

- **Keep a food log.** Most weight-management programs will promote the classic technique of starting a food diary because it helps you remember what you ate. Fortunately, there are a lot of new, innovative, and creative ways to keep track of what you eat. You can use a camera to snap a picture, document it on a phone app, use a voice recorder on your laptop, e-mail yourself, or jot it down in a notebook.

- **Sense it.** Think for a moment about the best dessert you ever had. Now describe it to yourself. Use a lot of sensory descriptors—the aroma, the texture, and so forth. Using all of your senses when you eat can help you later to remember what you ate hours earlier. Take a close look at your food and state one word for each of these dimensions. Say you eat a croissant. Smell: sweet; taste: buttery; touch: flakey; sound: of knife spreading jam. Purposefully focusing on how the food tastes and smells helps to encode the experience deeper into your memory. You are more likely to eat less later, because you have a better recall of what you consumed (Higgs and Woodward 2009). In other words, you are more likely to think *Oh, I remember eating a brownie at lunch. I'd better not have a sweet now* instead of forgetting about the brownie altogether.

- **Use mnemonics.** The art of assisting the memory by using a system of rhymes, rules, phrases, diagrams, and acronyms can help some people. For example, if you ate a snack of toast, apple, and pears, use the acronym TAP to remember it.

- **Relate the food to information you already know.** For example, if you eat blueberries, take a moment to reflect on what they do for you—pump you full of antioxidants. Imagine a pump. Or create a short story about the blueberries.

- **Leave evidence of what you eat.** Let's say you snack on a bag of pretzels. Keep the bag instead of pitching it. This will remind you how much you ate.

#53
Minding the Inch

Many people who struggle with their eating suffer from camelona-sophobia. It's likely that you do too, even if you've never heard of it. Let me tell you a story that can help explain it. It's based on Bedouin folklore. Bedouins are a camel-raising, desert-dwelling Arab tribe (hence the root word "camel"). A man from this tribe was traveling across the desert on his camel. As night approached, he pitched his tent to protect him from the cold. His camel asked, "Master, please let me enter, I'm cold." The man answered no and went to bed.

During the night, the camel yelled into the tent, "Master, I'm cold! Can I please just put my nose in the tent?" To quiet the complaining camel, he said yes and then fell back into a deep sleep. A short while later, the camel asked, "Can I just put my front legs in the tent? They have to be warm to help me travel so far." The master muttered okay just to make the camel be quiet. It worked, but now he was getting uncomfortable because the tent was quite crowded. The next time the master woke, he realized that he was sleeping outside the tent. The master had been pushed out. The camel was now alone in the tent.

This story illustrates a common fear that many of my clients experience. It's the "If I give myself an inch, I'll take a mile" phenomenon. If you say okay to just one bite of cake, you believe that inevitably you'll eat the entire cake. Or if you have just a couple of chips, you'll eventually eat the entire bag. Or the ultimate fear: "If I let loose on my diet just a little or give myself permission to relax, I will totally lose all control." Another term for this is the "slippery slope."

The slippery slope is a thinking fallacy that many of us experience. There are two problems with this type of thinking. The first is that your mind wants to convince you that A = Z. So if A happens (I eat a bite of cake), then by a gradual series of small steps through B, C, … X, Y, eventually and absolutely it will lead to Z (I will eat the whole cake). Thus, if you don't want Z (eating the whole cake), then A shouldn't occur either. The second problem is lack of distinction. This makes A (eating a bite) the same as Z (eating the whole cake). But there is quite a bit of difference between a bite and the entire cake. It's like saying that there is no difference between a very short person and a tall person. At some point there is a line you draw to say A is distinctly different and doesn't have to be the same as Z.

Skill Builder: *Minding the Inch*

Learn to spot the common thinking fallacy of the "If I give myself an inch, I'll take a mile" phenomenon with food. Notice whether you are creating a chain of inevitable events in your mind before they even happen. Is your mind so focused on Z (eating a whole cake) that it misses that there are many steps in between, from A to B and B to C, et cetera? You have many opportunities to intervene. A doesn't have to be inexorably linked with Z. Label all the possible steps in between.

Mentally make a distinction between A and Z before you start. In the cake example, draw an imaginary line with your mind. Be mentally present inch by inch. The problem often comes when you zone out a little between A and Z. With each inch, make an active decision to take another bite or to stop. Think of each bite as one inch.

At the end of the day, however, giving yourself only an inch may be part of the problem. Just like putting only his nose in the tent in an attempt to stay warm didn't keep the camel toasty enough, you will need to discover how much would be really satisfying—and then stick to it.

#54
Minding Your Worries

An insincere and evil friend is to be more feared than a wild beast; a wild beast may wound your body, but an evil friend will wound your mind.

—Buddha

This saying succinctly captures how harmful a toxic relationship can be to your state of mind and sense of well-being. It's tough to be mindful when you are worried about what other people think of you. Perhaps you've asked, "If my body isn't really attractive, will people like me?"

It is true that many people often make their first judgments based on appearances. But real relationships are based on far more substantial connections. When you are truly mindful of your relationships, you examine people from a holistic approach. You are appreciative of all aspects of who they are. Mindfulness doesn't value the past or future. Rather, it values people for who they are in the present moment. Get in touch with your reactions and with what you sense and how you feel in a friend's presence, as opposed to what you know about his past or what you think about who he'll be in the future.

People with eating issues are often people pleasers. People pleasers care a lot about making others happy, often at the expense of their own well-being. People pleasing inhibits mindfulness because you are always anticipating how people will react as opposed to being fully present and making decisions based on what you sense and feel in the moment.

Skill Builder: *Relationship Check*

If you worry about what other people think about your body, start by evaluating the quality of your relationships. Do you judge other people exclusively on their appearance? If you are critical of yourself, do you project this negativity onto other people and assume that this is what they think about you? Consider how this might affect your relationships. What is it that you are afraid others will see if they really know you?

When you are with friends and family, really be *with* them. Look in their eyes, touch their hands, keep your mind focused on the conversation. Take note of the feelings and thoughts that arise within you.

Skill Builder: *Mindful Body Talk*

Be more aware of the messages you receive from and send to your friends. The Buddha said, "Thousands of candles can be lighted from a single candle, and the life of the candle will not be shortened. Happiness never decreases by being shared." Don't make fat-phobic comments, check out others' bodies, or snicker about others' weight. Refuse to engage in disparaging talk about someone else's looks. When you find yourself giving someone the once-over and making a critical comment, counter it with a positive observation. Genuinely compliment others.

Try not to comment on changes in people's weight. You don't know what your comment may mean to someone, and you have no idea what kind of effect your comment may have on that person. Dieters often report mixed feelings on compliments for weight loss. They like the validation. Yet they wonder, "Was I really that bad before?" Your comments (both positive and negative) about weight can trigger an unintended reaction. For example, unhealthy, even dangerous, mindless undereating can be reinforced by well-meaning loved ones and coworkers who say, "Oh, you look so thin" or "You don't need to lose weight." If you must say something, use a generalized compliment like, "You look really nice today." Don't emphasize weight. Saying that someone looks "fat" or has "gained weight" can be very cruel. Value people not for their butts, thighs, or stomachs but for their hearts and minds.

#55
Mindful Practice

Fall down seven times, get up eight.

—Zen Proverb

This is a Buddhist saying about resilience, persistence, and the ability to bounce back. If you read biographies about the lives of successful millionaires, their stories are remarkably similar. These millionaires had a series of dramatic setbacks or failures. For example, Milton Hershey, the founder of Hershey's chocolate, went bankrupt several times before making his fortune. The one quality that set such successful people apart from others, and contributed to their eventual success, was their ability to accept loss, feel the pain, learn from the experience, and jump right back up. In a similar way, mindful eating takes practice, and, in the beginning, you may not always succeed. You need a strong resilience when your mind says, "I blew it! Why try to change my eating? It will never work."

As Buddha said, "A jug fills drop by drop." In other words, mindful eating is a continual journey that requires an enormous amount of persistence. Healing your eating habits could be a lifelong activity. Also, regardless of how well you master mindfulness, it will be impossible to escape an unintentional bout of mindless eating, or the occasional lapse into old undereating habits. The doughnuts at work, the pizza ordered in, or a food that induces guilty feelings will temporarily tempt you back into a nonaware, self-indulgent mind-set. When you realize what you have done, don't fall for the "Oh, well, I've completely ruined it anyway" attitude.

Expect the occasional out-of-the-blue mindless eating. It will happen. In fact, it would actually be a bad sign if problematic moments didn't occur. Sometimes, you need to eat mindlessly to reestablish contact with mindful eating. Mindless eating will remind you of the benefits of controlled, aware eating. Think of a bout of mindless eating as stepping into a pothole in the road. Consider it a challenge and tell yourself to keep walking. Think about it as if you were stepping out for a walk with a general, not specific, destination in mind. As the Buddha said, "If we are facing in the right direction, all we have to do is keep on walking."

Learning to become mindful is a way of thinking that develops over time. Instead of saying a task has been done "well" or "poorly," conscientious thinkers consider a deed as having been done in a "skillful" or "unskillful" manner. This acknowledges individual abilities and recognizes that what is right for one person may not be so for another. Remember that learning how to eat mindfully is a gradual process. It can be likened to earning different belt colors when learning a martial art. The skills build upon each other. You start at the beginning wearing a white belt, and you earn new belt colors by mastering different sets of skills. The black belt is the goal signifying mastery, but the student works slowly through a variety of different belt colors before achieving that goal.

Skill Builder: *Mindful Practice*

When you get discouraged, think:

- Progress, not perfection.

- I can take charge of this moment, not the future or the past.

- Make *now* a nonregrettable moment.

- Find true comfort, not momentary pleasure.

Remember that mindful eating takes time and practice. It won't happen overnight. Stay with it!

Part V

mindful eating motivations

This section is newly written for the second edition. The idea came about to provide readers with one place to turn to for quick inspiration, to help you switch gears, to get you on track to mindful eating. Emotional eaters will find the Checklist for Emotional Eaters chock-full of simple but effective tips to help you practice awareness while eating. A separate list of mindful eating quotations will motivate you when you need extra support. Finally, tips for practicing the four foundations of mindfulness are broken down into handy, concise segments.

Checklist for Emotional Eaters

This list of 59 mindful eating tips can be quickly and easily applied to your breakfast, lunch, and dinner. These handy tips are aimed to make you more attentive to *how* you eat. Refer to them anytime you feel that you may be slipping into mindless eating. Any action that makes you more aware of your food choices is one that brings you closer to mindful eating.

_____ **Solve the hunger mystery.** How do you know it's emotional rather than physical hunger? Ask yourself what happens if you say no to yourself, for instance, "No, ice cream is not a good idea." Do you throw a silent temper tantrum? Get angry? Feel it is unfair? If you say, "But I want it!" you know that this is likely to be an emotionally driven request to eat, rather than filling physical hunger. When you are physically hungry, you are often open to many foods to quiet the stomach. If you suspect emotional hunger, but aren't truly sure, tell yourself no as if you are firmly setting boundaries with a child asking for candy in a candy store. Notice whether you react with emotion or logic.

_____ **Chew gum.** If you struggle with emotional overeating or feeling hungry all the time, even after you eat, try chewing gum. According to a study in the journal *Appetite*, chewing gum for at least 45 minutes can reduce your appetite, make you feel less hungry for snacks, and increase fullness (Hetherington and Regan 2011). This is *not* to help you restrict your eating. Instead, chewing gum gives you an activity to do while you tune in to your body and observe what you are feeling and thinking.

_____ **Prevent roaming.** Another cue that you are one step away from mindless eating is roaming. You may notice yourself listlessly wandering around the kitchen, opening up a cabinet, peaking in without really looking, and then shutting it and repeating the steps with the refrigerator. If this is the case, sit down. Imagine being glued to your seat. Take a time-out to think clearly about what you are looking for. Are you in need of food or stress relief?

_____ **Decipher physical hunger.** Check out the acronym GET: **G**radually increasing desire for food versus the urge coming on suddenly, **E**mptiness in stomach (growling, rumbling, etc.), **T**iming (last meal or snack eaten approximately three hours ago). Ask yourself if it is time to GET food.

_____ **Feed the right need.** Put feelings and hunger in separate corners. If emotions are driving you to eat, be very specific about what you are feeling. Name the emotion very clearly. This will help you to find the right solution. For example, eating a sandwich or reading a book probably will not ease anger. But calling a friend to vent will do the trick.

_____ **Reverse hindsight for foresight.** Ask someone after the fact why she ate too many brownies and she is often able to explain it quite clearly. "I ate the brownies because I was just bored." Thus, the insight is there within you. However, the understanding often isn't accessed until after the fact, when it is too late. Take just one mindful moment ahead of time to ask yourself, "Why am I going to eat this brownie?" It doesn't matter if you are "right" or "wrong." Just take a stab at a reason. If you hear yourself answering, "I just want it," be sure to push yourself to thinking more deeply. This kind of reply is sidestepping the question.

_____ **Turn mindless picking into mindful choosing.** It's easy to pick mindlessly at a bowl of chips or to automatically scoop up a second helping of baked beans. It may even feel like your hand has a mind of its own. Your fingers just reach out without any real thought. To turn this around, focus your attention onto the placement of your hands and body. Pay close attention to how your body is positioned and watch it closely. If you find that you naturally gravitate back to the table or to an area where the snacks are kept, imagine that you are wearing a lead vest (the kind you would wear for an X-ray) or that you are walking underwater. Notice how these sensations slow down your automatic and sometimes unconscious movements. If your hand likes to pick at food, imagine wearing a heavy bracelet or watch. Or wear one as a reminder to be mindful of your movements.

_____ **Energize mindfully.** Some emotional eating is the result of being overly tired. Consider whether you are eating to wake up or get an energy boost. The obvious intervention is to get more sleep: take a short nap. If this doesn't work or you can't squeeze it in, try a few energizing exercises. Jogging or stepping in place quickly can get your blood pumping again. Caffeinated black tea rather than coffee or soda can be helpful; it helps to reduce your cortisol levels, the stress hormone that often leads you to stress eat, and it is soothing. However, in the long run, it is helpful to notice whether you use food to cope with fatigue and then find ways to get more rest.

_____ **Wind down mindfully.** One of the most common times of the day when people struggle with mindless emotional overeating is right after work. As soon as you walk in the door, you make a beeline for the kitchen. Sometimes it is hunger. But, in actuality, this is often just a way to unwind and relax. This makes a good case for finding a healthy way to detach from work. This may be something like taking five minutes to close your eyes at your desk before rushing out the door. Or turn down an extra side road to give yourself time to listen to a soothing song before you go home. You might also try changing your clothes as soon as you walk in the door to help shift out of work mode and to feel comfortable. If you are genuinely hungry, take a snack to eat before you leave the office. This gives your body twenty minutes for your brain to register that you ate and turn down the intensity of hunger when you walk in the door.

_____ **Use a napkin.** Switching gears from the fast pace of everyday life to a mindful mind-set at the dinner table can feel like turning on a dime. Place a napkin on your lap. Spread it out slowly. As you do so, turn your attention to the color of the napkin and the weight of it sitting on your lap. Imagine tucking all the issues on your mind under this napkin. Only when you are mentally and physically present and attentive to the table should you begin eating. Use the napkin in a ritualistic way to shift your mental state.

_____ **Disobey your inner food critic.** We all have a food critic living inside of our heads. Your inner food critic makes decisions about what to eat and what not to eat. To avoid getting caught up in his demands, learn to *hear* not *heed* his every wish. Just because you *think it* doesn't mean you have to *do it*. So if your mind says eat, acknowledge that message and know that you don't have to obey every command of your food critic.

_____ **Cook just enough.** A significant amount of mindless eating happens after dinner. Why? It becomes part of the clean-up ritual. You tell yourself, "If I just take another bite of the garlic bread I don't have to put it in a container or throw it away." Downsizing your cooking is an easier way to address this than trying to avoid picking at those leftovers. Try it out for an evening. If there are four people eating, make only four servings, not enough for extra portions or servings. This isn't to deprive you of food but to break the cycle of mindless overeating. If you want more later, you can always make additional servings. Or pack up your leftovers right away. Keep your mind focused on the fact that you will have less lunch tomorrow if you consume this now.

____ **Resist the magnetic force.** Many of my clients describe the pull to eat as being like a magnetic force. For instance, let's say there is a bag of chips in the cupboard. You take out a handful and then walk away. Then you munch on the chips, and when you finish you gravitate back to the same spot, take a handful, and walk away again. This cycle may repeat numerous times. This is a sign of emotional eating. Get out of the kitchen. Stay out. Go for a walk.

____ **Take a mental break.** Mindless eating sometimes plays the role of stalling and procrastinating. Do you use eating, which feels purposeful, as a way to avoid or delay an undesirable task, such as washing your dishes or doing your homework? Instead of eating, give yourself permission to take a five-minute mental break. At the end of the five minutes, reevaluate whether you are ready to tackle the task or whether you need to take another five. It's more helpful in the long run to give yourself permission to relax than to overeat.

_____ **Be wary of the slippery slope.** Be mindful of the activities that inevitably slide you right into mindless eating. Does going to a Mexican restaurant inevitably lead to overeating on tortilla chips? Perhaps nine times out of ten you buy a box of doughnuts instead of selecting just one. Avoid the inner battle with pastries by not going down the slippery slope in the first place. In other words, steer clear of the bakery or restaurant until you feel more confident. Make a list of events that seem linked with taking the slippery slope.

_____ **Be aware when eating socially.** Most people tend to mirror the way their friends, significant others, and family members eat. If you do this, don't be too hard on yourself. It often happens unconsciously. Be watchful. Notice whether you are matching your dining companion bite for bite. If so, try to stagger your bites. Notice their pace and try to downshift to picking up your fork just a little slower.

_____ **Have a snack before a meal.** Getting too hungry can cause mindless overeating. Before you get to an extreme level of hunger (shakiness, headache, low energy, etc.), choose a healthy snack. Purposefully electing to mindfully eat now can help you from overeating later. Picking a healthy snack is like an insurance policy against eating too much at the next mealtime.

_____ **Reassess portions.** It's okay to snack. You may just need to find ways to get a handle on your portion sizes. Get a muffin tin with six holes (or just use cupcake liners). When you want a snack, fill up one, two, or three of these holes depending on your hunger level. This can help you to visually see your portion sizes. The muffin tin also makes a great tray.

_____ **Snack consistently.** Get into a groove with your snacking routine by designating one particular bowl as your "snack bowl." Make it small, and put in it whatever you want to munch on. This will help you to consistently eat the same amount.

_____ **Practice gauging your hunger and fullness.** Getting to know your hunger and fullness signs is a critical task in mindful eating. Try practicing knowing what a full stomach feels like when you are in a good mood. Don't try to do it when you are struggling. Rate your level of hunger from 1 to 10, with 1 being extremely hungry and 10 being extremely full. Next, drink a glass of flat or carbonated water and rate your hunger and fullness again. Continue to drink the liquid. Notice different levels of fullness. You may want to repeat this exercise at different times of the day and when you are in different moods. Does your mood make it more difficult to identify how full you are?

_____ **Think SOS.** Lack of Sleep, unhealthy Substances, and Stress constitute a recipe for emotional overeating. Feeling tired, being overly stressed, and drinking or using drugs can make your body work at a subpar level. On an SSS day, think SOS: Safe place (choose the safest environment possible to reduce the risk of mindless eating), Observe (watch how these conditions impact your mood and ability to eat mindfully), calm your Senses (focus on soothing your senses by sleeping, placing a warm washcloth on your face, reading a distracting book, meditating, etc.).

____ **Plan mindfully.** We often mindlessly defer to our cravings like a child playing follow the leader. To break this autopilot behavior, before you leave the house always make a flexible plan for what you are going to eat for the rest of the day. This gives you an opportunity to throw a snack in your bag or to gather the resources necessary to prevent mindless eating later. It's helpful to always have a snack handy. We tend to eat whatever is near us when we feel desperate. This is when vending machines and fast food suck us in. Better to have a snack that you choose in advance than an impulse choice.

____ **Localize snacking.** When people try to quit smoking, they often limit their behavior to one particular area, such as on their front step, the outdoor smoking lounge at work, or in their car. This permits the behavior but localizes it to reduce other variables. It also reduces the ease and comfort of the behavior. Try the same with snacking. Permit yourself to snack but in an area that is out of the kitchen and a little inconvenient. This way, you won't eat mindlessly—and you may have to think twice about if you really want to snack.

____ **Take baby steps.** Dieting is like trying to empty a big pool in a matter of minutes. Mindful eating is emptying the pool one bucket at a time. What's a good small step? Try leaving just one or two bites on your plate. Small, mindful steps matter.

_____ **Get ready.** If your mind keeps telling you, "I want to eat healthfully but I can't right now," that is okay. Honor that feeling. Instead, ask yourself, "What can I do to prepare for when I am ready? … Chop up some veggies for later? Get my exercise clothes out? Pack a snack bag?"

_____ **Play detective.** If you aren't sure if you're hungry, scan your body for cues. Start with your toes and end at the top of your head. As you turn your attention to each body part, identify how it feels in this moment. Then ask yourself if hunger is located in that spot. For example, "Is hunger located in my feet?" You might answer, "In part, yes. I notice myself walking around searching for something to eat." This exercise serves two purposes. First, it helps you to get familiar with your body and to better read the signals when you are genuinely hungry. Second, it is a distraction.

_____ **Regulate your blood sugar.** One of the best ways to prevent emotional eating is sometimes to eat—or, rather, eat particular foods that will keep your blood sugar level steady. Whole grains, vegetables, and some fruits prevent spikes in your blood sugar (caused by candy and chocolate, for example) and subsequent crashes, which cause moodiness. These foods keep your blood sugar steadier, which helps prevent a cycle of emotional eating. Pay close attention to how your mood shifts after eating certain foods. Take note fifteen minutes after you eat. Check back in one hour later. What do you notice?

___ **Reassess mealtimes.** Do you eat at the same time each day no matter whether you are hungry or not? Maybe you eat during your favorite TV show each night. For one week, notice whether you set your eating schedule according to the clock. Shaking up your regular routines can help you break this cycle. For example, walk your dog before breakfast instead of afterward. Record your favorite TV show and watch it earlier in the day when you don't typically eat. The goal is to eat more according to your hunger than what is designated "dinnertime."

___ **Keep healthy foods in sight.** Think for a moment about where you store healthy foods. It's easy to forget about them when you can't see them. So keep healthy snacks within your sight path—on your desk, in a bowl on your counter, in a basket by the front door to grab as you leave. Revamp your refrigerator. Place healthy foods right up front, not out of sight in the vegetable drawer, where you will never see them.

___ **Be mindful of the mood-food connection.** What are you in the mood for? Do you ask yourself this every day? Rephrase this to ask yourself, "What food would satisfy my hunger?" The rule is that what you eat should be based on your hunger, not your mood.

___ **Eat like an athlete.** Athletes think about food from a very different perspective than most people. When they pick up a piece of food, they see it as energy. Before you eat, ask yourself whether the food is marathon-worthy (will fuel you for long time), best for jogging (will fuel you until your next meal), or great for a sprint (will give you a very quick burst of energy). Consider how long this food will keep you going and energized.

_____ **Love it or leave it.** Stop mindlessly munching on mediocre food by focusing on eating only those treats that you dearly love, not just like a little. Eat only desserts and treats that are a 9 or 10 on your pleasure list. Some clients agree to eat only treats that are truly unique or homemade. Maybe for you it is passing up any treats that aren't cheesecake.

_____ **Think comfort not pleasure.** Is your first reaction to stress the desire for sensory pleasure on the tongue to make things better? When you notice the urge to stress eat, think *comfort* not pleasure. What kinds of things bring comfort? Sleep, a fragrant candle, a pair of sweat pants, a soothing cup of tea, a hot bath? For more ideas, see my book *50 Ways to Soothe Yourself without Food.*

_____ **Create stopping points.** Packaged foods often have a natural stopping point built into them. These are the places where you stop to ask yourself, "Do I want more?" For example, the stopping point for a container of sandwich cookies is typically at the end of a row. For a bag of chips, it might be the bottom of the bag. These built-in stopping points often come too late, however.

To avoid bingeing, you may need to create your own. You can do so by putting food into smaller baggies. The bottom of the baggy creates a new stopping point. When you are done with the bag, tune in to your stomach. Ask yourself, "Do I want or crave more? Or am I content?"

_____ **Eat something new.** Are you afraid of ordering a new dish or eating unfamiliar healthy foods? Don't be. Tell yourself, "For just this meal, I will investigate what happens if I don't eat onion rings." Or "I will order something different for dinner just this once." This challenge doesn't lock you into a long-term commitment. Use this trial to see what new sensations and feelings pop up.

_____ **Recalibrate your palate.** Do you desire foods that are extremely sweet? Do you dislike healthy foods? That may be because many processed foods are hundreds of times sweeter than natural foods. So our taste buds become skewed by flavors that are exaggerated and not naturally occurring. Eating whole foods can help your tongue to be satisfied with healthier, natural foods. As you decrease your intake of sugar and salt, your palate changes and your sensitivity to these items increases. Try to eat foods that are grown locally and are fresh—thus not packed with artificial flavorings, preservatives, added sugar, extra salt, et cetera.

_____ **Consider your carbon footprint.** What you eat doesn't just impact you, it has a ripple effect on the environment and the entire world. This is not to produce guilt but to help you to take a step back from your plate. What you eat also impacts those around you—from your spouse to someone halfway across the world. If you can't get motivated, take a moment to pause before you eat. Look closely at what is on your plate. Consider where all the items came from. A local farm? Another state? Another country? Before you eat a banana, check the sticker to see where it is from.

_____ **Move mindfully.** If the word "exercise" makes you cringe, stop using this triggering word. Instead, focus on *movement*. Sign up for a local one-mile walk, or run a 5K (or more, if you already have experience) for a charity—breast cancer, autism, diabetes, you name it. If you don't have a cause you support, look on the National Eating Disorders website (see Resources) for national walks. Committing to an organized event has many benefits. It moves you into training mode, gives you a measurable and definable goal, and sets a permanent end date.

_____ **Calm down your body.** Stress-driven eating is, in part, spurred by the physiological reaction you have when you are upset. Your body shifts into the fight-or-flight response. If you feel the urge to stress eat, try out some different ways to calm down your body: take several deep breaths, stretch, take a time-out, practice self-massage, reduce extra stimulation (like turning down the music or lights). Calm down all of your senses. Then reevaluate if you want to eat.

_____ **Dine rather than eat.** Consider for a moment *how* you eat, particularly things like fast food. Do you eat them out of a paper bag? Standing up over the sink? Out of a box? To shift into a mindful eating mode, put down a place mat or use a nice plate. This can help to remind you that eating is important, special, and deserves all of your attention.

_____ **Can vs. can't.** Is your mind constantly saying, "I can't eat that!"? If so, you may be triggering more mindless eating than preventing it. Continually wagging your finger at yourself can cause you to sneak food or feel a sense of deprivation. Instead, orient your mind to looking at food with an "I can eat it" attitude. Remind yourself that it is a choice. "I choose to eat it or I choose not to eat it." Remember that it is better to make a conscious decision to eat mindlessly than to make the decision unconsciously.

_____ **Practice gratitude.** Before you take a bite, take a moment to appreciate the food in front of you. Think about where it came from and all it took to get to your plate. Say a short prayer or simply say, "Thank you." Gratitude can shift your mind into an appreciative, mindful mode.

_____ **Make a choosemyplate.org place mat.** Not sure what your plate should look like? In 2011, the government nixed the food pyramid and put together a tool that can help you to become a more mindful eater. Rather than specific amounts, the icon shows you helpful portion ratios. Print out the photo and make it into a place mat.

_____ **Believe in change.** Many people want to change but secretly don't believe even for a second that anything can be different. Imagine yourself eating mindfully— eating when you are hungry and stopping when you are full. Visualize yourself doing something you believe is impossible for you to do, like eating just one cookie or cooking a healthy meal. If you "see" yourself doing it, you can!

_____ **Heed internal cues.** Why do you stop eating? Notice whether you use internal or external cues. External cues are things like the waitress taking your plate away (implying you are done), the bag is finished, it's time to return to work. Internal cues are feeling satisfied by food or noticing that your thoughts are saying stop or "I'm finished." Notice whether you lean on external or internal cues to know when to stop and start eating. Direct your attention to internal cues. These are much more accurate in helping you to know when to put your fork down.

_____ **Turn it inside out.** Many of my clients struggle with open containers of food. It might be an open bag of chips or a plastic container of leftovers. Once the lid is off, it is often difficult to stop eating until there's nothing left. You might notice that your hand keeps entering the open bag. If this sounds like you, do an experiment. Open up the container and pour out all the contents onto a paper towel. Notice how different the food looks laid out this way. This alters the process of eating it. Looking at the entire amount all at once rather than by handfuls can help you eat a better portion size. Now try grabbing several baggies and divvying up the food into portions that you think would leave you contented.

_____ **Change your aim.** Aim to remove hunger, rather than feeling satisfied or full. You've likely been trained to think that "feeling full" ends the meal. If you are waiting for this cue, you are likely putting yourself at high risk for mindless eating. Learn to look for feeling *okay* instead of *full*.

_____ **Think about dessert first.** Do you eat dinner and then ask, "Do I have room for dessert?" You typically have to be pretty full to turn down a dessert, right? Sometimes it is helpful to put the cart before the horse. Consider first whether you want dessert and then adjust your eating accordingly. Don't *find* room for dessert, *make* room.

_____ **Avoid black-and-white thinking.** Nothing railroads you into overeating like extreme thinking. Whenever you hear yourself saying, "I've blown it completely!" or other sentences that start with "I should" or "I always" or "I can't ever do that," keep a thought log. Notice how many times you make all-or-nothing decisions about food. Aim for more neutral ways of speaking about your eating. Staying away from absolutes is a helpful practice for life in general.

_____ **Be realistic.** Emotional eaters often unknowingly set themselves up for guilt and disappointment. They set their expectations way too high with glorious and grand promises, such as, "I won't eat any junk food ever again." If you constantly feel like you are disappointing yourself, make your expectations more realistic. Consider what you actually do now and challenge yourself just a little. If you typically eat three cookies, aiming for two may be more realistic than one or none.

_____ **Get out of the food coma.** Emotional eating often wipes out all feeling. It can make you numb as if you were shot with anesthetic, shutting off the thoughts, feelings, and sensations that would otherwise force you to deal with the issue at hand. When you slip into a food coma, you don't feel anything. But you also don't hear your thoughts saying stop or feel the fullness in your stomach. If you notice that you are feeling nothing, give yourself a gentle pinch to help yourself be awake and present. Pay attention to the sensation. It is likely to be slightly uncomfortable. Notice how this shifts your awareness. Go back to eating mindfully.

_____ **Flip a coin.** Can't decide whether to eat something or not? If so, eliminate your food struggle by flipping a coin (call heads or tails), throwing a single die (1–3 means you eat, 4–6 means you don't), or drawing a card (black card means you eat, red means you don't). Notice your reaction to having the decision made for you. What do you feel? Relief? Anger? Disappointment? Rebellion? This feeling is important because it gives you a lot of information about what you are struggling with. Explore that.

_____ **Remove distractions.** In a recent study, subjects who were distracted by playing solitaire during lunch were less full after they ate than those who didn't play a game while they ate. They also ate significantly more than did participants who were not distracted (Oldham-Cooper et al. 2011). So keep distractions at bay to avoid overeating.

_____ **Ask yourself …** Finish this statement: If I eat _____, then I will feel _____. This technique can help you to get to the bottom of what emotion you are trying to soothe with food.

_____ **Minimize comfort eating.** If you find yourself continuing to gravitate toward comfort eating, reduce the negative impact of it. For instance, gnaw on a healthy snack, like carrots. Choose the healthiest, most satisfying option possible; if chocolate candy is your weakness, drink chocolate milk instead.

_____ **Take small bites.** Eat the thing you crave in slow, mindful bites. Eating at a slow rate can significantly reduce how much you eat, particularly for large meals (Scisco et al. 2011). To slow down between bites, see the skill builder Slowly but Surely, Decelerating Your Eating, from #3, Moment-to-Moment Eating.

_____ **Delay eating.** Promise yourself that you will eat the food you crave after doing something else for five minutes. You may find that your craving diminishes a bit or is gone in this time frame. This is a sign of an emotional rather than physical urge.

_____ **Stoke your senses.** Choose a food that dramatically changes your senses: try something hot, cool, spicy, crunchy, et cetera. Take note of how all parts of your body react to the sensations, from what you feel on your tongue to what you hear and smell. Repeat this with a different new food next week.

_____ **Use your slow cooker.** A lot of mindless eating happens at the end of long day, when you're tired. Having a wholesome meal done and ready for you come dinnertime will help keep you from reaching for unhealthy snacks or fast foods. Turn on the slow cooker after breakfast and you'll have dinner waiting for you in a few hours.

Mindful Eating Quotations

Words of wisdom can make a difference, particularly when you are having a challenging day. This collection of timeless advice all speaks to the same idea—that eating mindfully is good for your mental and physical health. Make a copy of these pages. Hang them up for inspiration!

"One cannot think well, love well, sleep well, if one has not dined well." —Virginia Woolf

"Tell me what you eat, and I will tell you who you are." —Anthelme Brillat-Savarin

"Let food be thy medicine, thy medicine shall be thy food." —Hippocrates

"Part of the secret of success in life is to eat what you like and let the food fight it out inside." —Mark Twain

"Better to eat a dry crust of bread with peace of mind than have a banquet in a house full of trouble." —Proverbs

"The more you eat, the less flavor; the less you eat, the more flavor." —Chinese proverb

"The spirit cannot endure the body when overfed, but, if underfed, the body cannot endure the spirit." —Saint Frances de Sales

"The doctor of the future will give no medication, but will interest his patients in the care of the human frame, diet and in the cause and prevention of disease." —Thomas A. Edison

"One should eat to live, not live to eat." —Benjamin Franklin

"When walking, walk. When eating, eat." —Zen proverb

"The way you cut your meat reflects the way you live." —Confucius

"Hunger is the best sauce in the world." —Cervantes

"He who distinguishes the true savor of his food can never be a glutton; he who does not cannot be otherwise." —Henry David Thoreau

"We load up on oat bran in the morning so we'll live forever. Then we spend the rest of the day living like there's no tomorrow." —Lee Iacocca

"Before eating, always take time to thank the food." —Arapaho proverb

"Eat not to dullness, drink not to elevation." —Benjamin Franklin

Top Ten Mindfulness Motivators

In this chapter, you will read quick tips that get right to the heart of being mindful of your mind, body, thoughts, and feelings. Use this section as a quick refresher. Keep these lists handy to read over daily.

Ten Ways to Practice Mindfulness of the Mind

1. **Observe.** Do nothing different. Just watch how you eat. Fast? Slow? Sitting? Standing? What time is it? Where are you?

2. **Take mindful bites.** Touch. Taste. Smell. Listen. Zoom in on each mouthful. Where is your mind during this bite? Zoned out not tasting a thing? Tuned in to each bite? Or somewhere in the middle?

3. **Quiz yourself.** Ask yourself before eating, "Am I physically or emotionally hungry right now?"

4. **Be in the moment.** Eat in a different way. Use chopsticks or your fingers instead of a fork. Sit in a different seat. Use the opposite hand. Choose a new food.

5. **Remove distractions.** Make one mindful meal a day—eat it without distraction. Turn off the TV. Put your book or computer aside.

6. **Categorize less.** Stop using food stereotypes and labels to make decisions. Rather than categorizing food as "good," "bad," "should," "shouldn't," consciously choose based on facts not feelings.

7. **Identify the origin of your hunger.** Get to the root of why you are eating. Are you avoiding something? Feeling stressed? Are you really hungry?

8. **Speak compassionately to yourself.** Be kind. This will help you to be honest with yourself.

9. **Start a food diary.** Raise your awareness by recording what you eat. Take a picture to create a photo journal. Or write it down.

10. **Let go of old dieting strategies.** Ask yourself with each bite, "Am I eating mindfully?"

Ten Ways to Practice Mindfulness of the Body

1. **Tune in.** When you are sitting still, tune in to your feet, hands, legs, neck. Do this during different times of the day. Notice and appreciate what it feels like to be hungry or full, still or moving, and so on. Scan your body. Be well acquainted with your body's different physical states.

2. **Measure your hunger level.** Check in with your hunger level several times a day. Ask yourself, "How hungry am I on a scale from 1 to 10?" with 1 being starvation and 10 being completely stuffed. Aim for a 5.

3. **Breathe.** Clear your mind. Take a deep breath. Count to ten as you inhale. Deep breaths can calm down stress, the kind that leads to emotional eating. Deep breathing can also shift you out of autopilot and jolt you out of an eating trance.

4. **Take cues from your body.** Listen to your body, not your emotional thoughts. When you overeat, your mind may focus on guilt. Tune in to the physical consequences. Heartburn? Feeling stuffed? Tired? You'll be more motivated to avoid uncomfortable sensations than guilty thoughts.

5. **Dress well.** Use your body as a helpful tool. Dress comfortably. Avoid tight clothing (which can trigger guilt

and frustration). Dressing up can make you feel good about yourself, which is a great motivator.

6. **Accept it.** You don't have to love your body, just accept it as it is. As hard as it is, list what you do appreciate about your body.

7. **Listen to what your body is telling you.** Before each bite, name specific bodily cues that let you know if you are emotionally or physically hungry. Stomach grumbling? Low energy? Empty feeling?

8. **Avoid the Clean Plate Club.** Intentionally leave a bite or two. Step out of the all-or-nothing mentality.

9. **Reassess the scale.** Understand your relationship with the scale. Some people step on the scale too much. They use it to reassure themselves or as a punishment. Other people avoid it, not wanting to be aware of where they are at in terms of weight. Observe how you use the scale and how it impacts your mood. Your favorite clothing can help you be aware without being as triggering as a number on the scale.

10. **Respond to cravings mindfully.** Listen to what your body wants. Try to work with your cravings instead of fighting them off. Better to eat a small piece of chocolate mindfully and consciously with planning than to try to wrestle away the desire and end up overeating or eating in a mindless trance.

Ten Ways to Practice Mindfulness of Feelings

1. **Make a trigger list.** Write down the feelings that lead you to eat. Joy? Stress? Anxiety?

2. **Investigate your feelings.** Ask yourself, "Am I eating because I am feeling _____?" What do you hope this food will make you feel?

3. **Creatively express your feelings.** Tell a friend. Draw a picture. Write about your emotions in a journal. Process your feelings.

4. **Clear your mind.** Take a deep breath in through your nose. Exhale. Count to ten as you let air out through your lips.

5. **Create a metaphor to explain how you feel.** When approaching mealtime, describe your feelings by saying something like "I feel like a squirrel gathering nuts and hiding them way." Visualize this metaphor.

6. **Assess your dining companions.** Notice whether your relationships hurt or help your efforts to eat mindfully. Make sure to avoid copying or mimicking the eating habits of those you dine with.

7. **Socialize without food.** A lot of bonding happens over food. Intentionally build in some socialization away from food. Go to a movie. Take a walk. Host game night. Meet for coffee.

8. **Put perfection out of your mind.** Nothing ever feel good enough? Your body? Your work? If so, get a handle on perfectionism by finding what is *realistic* rather than *perfect*.

9. **Beat boredom.** Set up a plan for what to do when you have five minutes, ten minutes, or an hour to fill up—without food. Be specific.

10. **Curb anger.** Anger can cause a significant portion of mindless eating. Find safe outlets for your anger. Call a friend to vent. Walk it off. Sleep on it.

Ten Ways to Practice Mindfulness of Thoughts

1. **Balance thinking versus being.** Clarify the difference between *thinking* you are hungry and *being* hungry. Notice the difference between thinking you are relaxed and being relaxed. Ask yourself, "Am I thinking that I am hungry or am I being hungry?"

2. **Think in shades of gray.** Notice when you've stepped into thinking quicksand. This is all-or-nothing thinking, worrying about the worst-case scenario, and making assumptions. Gently point it out to yourself.

3. **Have a healthy debate.** Imagine your healthy thoughts on one shoulder and unhealthy ones on the other. Encourage the thoughts to talk back and forth to each other. Externalize the debate about what to eat and what not to eat. Use facts not feelings (for instance, focus on the nutritional content versus your fear).

4. **Eat to be content.** Work toward a middle ground between the eating extremes—being not full or starving, just okay. Aim to feel content.

5. **Think "realistic."** When your mind wants to set your expectations too high (such as, "I won't eat any sweets today"), ask yourself, "What can I realistically do?"

6. **Choose among your thoughts.** Remember, you don't have to obey every one of your thoughts. Choose to let some thoughts go without thinking about them too

much. Let them pass like a car on the highway speeding past you.

7. **Use neutral words.** When reacting to food, try not to use positive or negative words. Stay in a neutral zone by saying words like okay, acceptable, fine, satisfactory, healthy, and so on, rather than good, bad, awful, love it, hate it.

8. **Practice visualizing.** Imagery is powerful. Visualize yourself often eating in a mindful way—passing up many treats, walking away from fast food, eating healthy snacks. Using imagery will make it much easier to do these things when you attempt them in real life.

9. **Talk back to your inner critic.** Internal criticism can try to rule your thoughts like a backseat driver. But criticism and guilt don't motivate you to change. Kind words do. Being kind to yourself helps you to be honest with yourself and take a candid look at your behavior. Use compassionate speech.

10. **Keep your thoughts in the present.** When they want to gravitate to the future or the past, bring them back to *right now*—what you are sensing, seeing, feeling, touching, tasting in this very minute. This can help you let go of feeling guilty or worrying that you will "mess up healthy eating."

Who Can Help You to Eat Mindfully?

Mastering mindful eating is no easy task. The more difficult it is for you to change your eating patterns and your mind-set, the more likely it is that you would benefit from professional assistance. Although friends and family can be extremely helpful, sometimes talking to them about weight issues is tricky. When you talk about your own weight concerns and fears, it is often difficult for friends or family members to be sufficiently detached from their own weight fears and anxieties to really listen to what you say.

If you are unable to change your eating habits independently, or if meditating on the issues underlying your problem eating brings up overwhelming emotional reactions, it is important to seek professional help. A professional can assess what other factors need to be addressed. Professional help can be had from psychologists, psychiatrists, physicians, nurses, and nutritionists. A team of professionals is highly recommended. Each professional brings specialized training to an aspect of the mind, body, thoughts, or feelings, which, woven together, creates a holistic treatment. A medical professional is particularly valuable because antidepressants or other medications are necessary for some individuals. Lots of options exist, including in-patient treatment for those who need to dedicate all of their attention at that moment.

Fluctuation in caloric intake is difficult on your mind and body. It can severely interfere with your concentration. A professional can tell you how to regain your focus. It is critical to seek additional help if you have mood issues or alcohol and/or drug problems. It is also critical if you are feeling suicidal, have had a dramatic loss of weight, are experiencing physical symptoms, or are acting impulsively. These symptoms are likely to severely inhibit mindful eating because of competing emotional demands.

Essentially, counseling is a way to break through your "stuck" thinking patterns. It helps you to articulate your feelings about food, and to identify patterns and connect the dots between the significant events in your life. As a counselor, I have guided many people through overcoming a wide range of eating issues. I feel honored by their trust and that they allowed me to help them combat their difficult problems.

When I think about my own role as a counselor, I imagine myself as a skydiving instructor. I am attached to the skydiver's back with an extra parachute just in case hers doesn't open. I allow the person to decide when she is going to jump, and how quickly she wants to open her own chute. I won't let her hit the ground, but I encourage all my clients to be mindfully in control. You may be afraid, and that's okay. I am sharing this image with you to let you know that professionals like me are here to help, not to judge, evaluate, or take away your control.

Practical Solutions for Everyday Mindless Eating Scenarios

Providing specific instructions on what to do in difficult moments was an extremely important part of this book for me to write. Typically, my clients gain extraordinary insight into the origins and meaning of their food issues when they begin to practice mindful eating. However, they repeatedly have the same complaint: "What specifically can I do when I'm *really* struggling?" The following scenarios walk you through some helpful steps. Refer back to the respective sections of the book for expanded descriptions of skill builders for each type of mindless eater.

Scenario 1: Mindless Overeating

You have been sitting alone in front of your desk for several hours working on a project. You begin to think about the stash of chocolate candy hidden in the bottom of your desk drawer. Instantly, you forget what you are working on and you can think about nothing but chocolate. In the past, opening up the desk drawer has led to uncontrolled, mindless eating.

Mindful Solutions

- **Pause.** Stop everything you are doing (put down your pen, disconnect the phone) and devote your full attention to this issue.

- **Breathe.** Slow down and do a quick breathing exercise. Focus and become aware of your body and your surroundings. Ask yourself what your breathing tells you about how you are feeling. Bring your attention to your breathing to re-center yourself and to increase your awareness.

- **Question your hunger.** Ask yourself, "Am I really hungry?" Be mindful of the physical cues and facts that help you decide whether you are or not. When was the last time you ate? What is your body telling you?

- **Find a different fuel.** If the answer is "No, I am not hungry," investigate your feelings. Are you feeling bored by work or anxious about the project you are working on? What is going on? What else can you do to deal with what you're feeling? Think about what might fill you up other than food. Will getting up from your desk and taking a short walk help? Is your body cramped from sitting still so long? Do you need to stretch? Would it help to call a friend or to talk to a coworker for a few minutes?

- **Question your cravings.** If the answer is, "Yes, I am hungry," think about your options. Identify what you really want to eat, and how much of it you need to satisfy your hunger.

- **Use your senses.** Tune in to all of your senses as you eat. Be in touch with the process of eating and with your body's reactions to the food. Take mindful bites.

- **Use imagery.** You know that starting to eat chocolate has led to a slippery slope of overeating in the past. Therefore, imagine a large yellow-and-black DANGER road sign blocking the handle of your desk drawer. Meditate on that image.

Scenario 2: Mindless Undereating

You've been trying to lose weight and therefore skipped breakfast this morning. Your stomach is rumbling, and your head is beginning to throb. Although you would like to eat something, many thoughts stream through your mind, like "You're too fat to eat." You struggle between listening to your stomach and the judgmental voice inside your head.

Mindful Solutions

- **Don't wait too long between meals.** If your stomach is grumbling, think of this as a huge red neon sign flashing, "I need food." When your stomach makes noise, that means you've waited too long. This puts you at greater risk of mindless eating. Stop what you are doing and focus completely on the physical cues your body is sending you. Be aware and observe. Take note of the sensations that you are feeling, for next time. They will let you know you are really hungry. Breathe.

- **Reconnect.** Prevent yourself from going overboard. Carefully make a plan by thinking about what would be good for your body and what you need at this moment. Spend time being inside your body and understanding what it needs. Watch your thoughts as outlined in #19, Meditation: Studying Your Body's Cues Mindfully.

- **Curb judgmental thoughts.** Listen to the comments going through your mind. Notice your thoughts and feelings as you become aware of them. When they occur, label them for what they are, as "just a thought" or "just a feeling." If you are launching a personal attack on yourself, stop and instead think about the physical and emotional consequences of your actions. Transform your judgmental language into calm, soothing words. Talk yourself through it.

- **Be compassionate.** Speak kindly to yourself. Consider what you would tell someone else. If you have difficulty being sympathetic to yourself, call someone who will be. Avoiding criticism will help you to examine the situation with an open, mindful stance.

- **Question what else is happening.** Examine the larger context of what is going on in this moment. Clearly, you are hungry, but what else is going on internally? Think about what happened in the events surrounding this moment. Think first about the present moment, and then think deeply about your feelings in the preceding moments. What prompted this struggle?

- **Accept yourself.** Eating can induce many negative feelings about yourself and your body. In this moment, acknowledge that at some level you simply must accept your body as it is. You are in control of making that choice. You don't have to love every aspect of your body to respect it and treat it well. Think about how the food is going to enhance how well your body functions. Your headache will stop. Use imagery to imagine where the food will travel once it is inside.

Scenario 3: Mindless Chaotic Eating

A group of friends get together one night at your home to watch a movie and eat a pizza. They order your favorite pizza toppings. Everyone is eating several slices, which leads you to eat two more pieces than you typically would have eaten. After they leave, you eat another slice, despite not being hungry. You begin to feel the urge to rid yourself of the heavy pizza and the too-full feeling.

Mindful Solutions

- **Forgive and accept.** When you lapse back into mindless eating, it may feel as if you are beginning your journey all over again or, even worse, that you have completely strayed off the path. This is not true. Once you've learned about mindfulness, you won't forget it. It's a matter of reapplying principles. At this point, you need to forgive yourself. Most people advocate for "forgive and forget." Mindfulness doesn't do that. Instead, it urges you to "forgive and accept." Don't try to push away your feelings. Accept all that you are feeling.

- **Investigate.** Feeling too full is a common reason people get the urge to eliminate their food. A much healthier way to deal with the uncomfortable feelings is to dig deeper into the feelings. Stop and meditate on the emotional components of your bodily feelings. Getting in touch with your feelings will be useful for preventing overeating next time.

- **Uncover binge triggers.** The urge to purge the food is a quick way of dealing with the anxiety that is aroused by eating unnecessary calories. It is important to be mindful and to meditate on the entire evening. What feelings prompted you to eat mindlessly, particularly after your friends left? What tends to trigger eating when you aren't even hungry? Is this a pattern?

- **Understand the physical consequences.** Purging is instigated by the negative emotions that arise when you realize you ate mindlessly. Purging is dangerous. When individuals first begin purging, they are more aware of their negative feelings and their body's physical reactions. Over time, the individual disconnects from the moment-to-moment discomfort of purging and anticipates feeling better, soothed, or relieved that the extra calories are gone. Acknowledge what purging does to your body in a nonjudgmental way.

- **Redirect activity.** The urge to feel better quickly by purging the food is tempting and sometimes feels difficult to control. Therefore, it is important to refocus your mind on other things. Get out of the house. Take a walk, listen to music, or visit someone. Find a soothing activity to engage in that will help you reduce your anxiety about the entire experience.

Scenario 4: Stepping Back in the Midst of Temptation

You are in your kitchen and are wrestling with the temptation to reach for a bag of cookies sitting on the shelf. You think, "I just want one taste." But you fear you may eat the whole bag.

Mindful Solutions

- **Step back:** Imagine yourself actively taking a step back from the situation. Why is stepping back important?

When stressed or overwhelmed, people tend to revert to autopilot. This means eating or behaving in their habitual way. Essentially, you react automatically rather than investigating all the pertinent and critical information. Stepping back helps you to obtain, thoughtfully and consciously, all the information you need to identify an array of solutions. Stepping back is carefully responding with diligent thought rather than robotically reacting. Identify how you would typically react.

- **Say it.** Describe aloud what is happening to you both internally and externally. Use detail, description, and lots of adjectives. Rely on your senses: sight, smell, sound, taste, and touch. Use vivid details, as if you were describing the scene to someone with his eyes closed. For example, say, "I really want a cookie. I'm in the kitchen standing in front of the cabinet. I am afraid I am going to overeat and finish all the cookies in the box. I feel nervous, and my hands are shaking. I'm sweating with anxiety, and I'm pacing around because I don't know what to do."

- **Involve your sixth sense.** The sixth and most important sensory organ is your mind. Describe what you are feeling and thinking. Think about the situation objectively without inserting any judgmental statements. Don't distort the description with statements that what is happening is "bad" or "wrong." Be compassionate with yourself. For instance, say, "I feel really hungry, and I am frustrated. This is a really tough situation for me. In the past, I know, this kind of situation has ended up with me feeling really bad. It's okay to feel this way."

- **State what you want.** Verbalizing clearly is like translating a foreign text into your own language. Read the situation, pause, and describe it using your own words. For example, say, "I want to eat a cookie, but I don't want to binge or overeat. How do I feel? This really stinks!"

- **Think ahead.** Describe your options. Consider every scenario. You might say, "I could binge. Or I could leave the room, eat something else, have one cookie and stop, call someone, watch TV, or go for a walk."

- **Describe your choice.** Make a decision. Visualize that decision. Imagine carrying out your decision. Then say it aloud, such as "I will eat just one and leave the kitchen to prevent myself from eating too many." Close your eyes and picture yourself walking out of the room.

- **Let go.** Describe what you need to release. You might say, "I may not feel completely satisfied in the moment, but I will feel better about myself after the urge subsides."

Resources

Mindfulness Websites

dukeintegrativemedicine.org

Duke Integrative Medicine mindfulness classes, workshops, and seminars.

eatingmindfully.com

Mindful eating tools, event information, free handouts, a newsletter, and research information. Great for the general public and for therapists. I announce my speaking events and workshops on this site.

emindful.com

A company that has partnered with some of the world's leading researchers in the rapidly growing field of mindfulness. Health and wellness services listed.

eomega.org

Through innovative educational experiences that awaken the best in the human spirit, Omega provides hope and healing for individuals and society.

www.fitwoman.com

Green Mountain offers an intelligent, pragmatic, non-diet program developed during four decades of working with women in order to help them find and maintain their natural, healthy weight.

geneenroth.com

Geneen Roth is the author of eight groundbreaking, inspiring books on compulsive eating and perpetual dieting.

www.intuitiveeating.org

The web companion to *Intuitive Eating*, by Evelyn Tribole, MS, RD, and Elyse Resch, MS, RD, FADA. Innovative, groundbreaking approach for balanced eating.

www.kripalu.org

Yoga and mindfulness retreats for beginners and advanced individuals.

marc.ucla.edu

University of California Los Angeles Mindful Awareness Research Center. Download free meditations, mindfulness research, and resources.

mindful.org

A website dedicated to giving voice, inspiration, guidance, and connection to all those who want to enjoy the proven benefits of mindfulness practices and to create a more mindful and caring society.

www.mindfuleating.net

Basic overview and information on mindful eating.

www.mindfulness-solution.com

Free mindfulness meditations, downloads, events, and programs by Dr. Ronald Siegel, a well-known mindfulness instructor and professor at Harvard Medical School.

www.mindfulselfcompassion.org

Site by Dr. Christopher Germer that offers mindfulness and self-compassion resources, downloads, and training events.

mindlesseating.org

Site for the book *Mindless Eating: Why We Eat More Than We Think*. Learn about Dr. Brian Wansink's award-winning academic research on changing eating behaviors. Resources and strategies to help you eat better are listed.

newharbinger.com

Help end the triggers of mindless eating by reading some of New Harbinger's hundreds of quality self-help books written by qualified professionals.

www.savorthebook.com

Web companion to *Savor: Mindful Eating, Mindful Life* by Thich Nhat Hanh and Lilian Cheung.

slowfoodusa.org

Slow Food USA is part of a global, grassroots organization with supporters in more than 150 countries who believe that food and farming should be sources of health and well-being for everyone.

tcme.org

TCME is a forum for professionals across all disciplines interested in developing, deepening, and understanding the value and importance of mindful eating.

www.umassmed.edu/cfm/index.aspx

The Center for Mindfulness in Medicine, Health Care, and Society is a visionary force and global leader in mind-body medicine.

www.yogajournal.com

New to yoga? Visit this site for a good introduction and for your continued practice.

www.zendust.org/zco/chozen-and-hogen-bays

Mindful Eating author Jan Chozen Bays is a teacher for the Zen Community of Oregon and a pediatrician.

Healthy Eating References

Resources to help you learn about nutrition, food safety, and obesity.

www.choosemyplate.org

www.cnpp.usda.gov/dietaryguidelines.htm

www.eatright.org

www.hsph.harvard.edu/nutritionsource

navigator.tufts.edu

www.nutrition.gov

www.thenutritionsource.org

www.yaleruddcenter.org

Eating Disorder References

www.aedweb.org

An international organization the supports research and treatment of eating disorders.

edreferral.com

Look here to find referrals to dieticians, therapists, and physicians who specialize in eating issues.

www.bulimia.com

A bookstore for quality books and resources on eating issues. The site also has information on treatment centers.

iaedp.com

The International Association of Eating Disorders Professionals provides quality education and high-level training standards to an international multidisciplinary group of various health-care treatment providers and helping professions, who treat the full spectrum of eating disorder problems.

www.nationaleatingdisorders.org

A national organization that supports and raises funds for prevention and treatment of eating disorders.

www.something-fishy.org

General information on eating disorders and disordered eating.

www.webmd.com

Find information on eating disorders and eating problems.

Books

Albers, Susan. 2011. *But I Deserve This Chocolate: The 50 Most Common Diet-Derailing Excuses and How to Outwit Them.* Oakland, Calif.: New Harbinger.

Albers, Susan. 2003. *Eat, Drink and Be Mindful.* Oakland, Calif.: New Harbinger.

Albers, Susan. 2009. *50 Ways to Soothe Yourself without Food.* Oakland, Calif.: New Harbinger.

Albers, Susan. 2006. *Mindful Eating 101.* New York: Routledge.

Altman, Don. 1998. *Art of the Inner Meal: Food for Thought and Spiritual Eating.* Los Angeles: Moon Lake Media.

Bays, Jan Chozen. 2009. *Mindful Eating: A Guide to Rediscovering a Healthy and Joyful Relationship with Food.* Boston: Shambhala.

Brantley, Jeffrey, and Wendy Millstine. 2009. *Five Good Minutes in Your Body: 100 Mindful Practices to Help You Accept Yourself and Feel at Home in Your Body.* Oakland, Calif.: New Harbinger.

Fain, Jean. 2011. *The Self-Compassion Diet: A Step-by-Step Program to Lose Weight with Loving-Kindness.* Boulder, Colo.: Sounds True.

Goodall, Jane. 2005. *Harvest for Hope: A Guide to Mindful Eating.* New York: Warner.

Heffner, Michelle, and George H. Eifert. 2004. *The Anorexia Workbook: How to Accept Yourself, Heal Your Suffering, and Reclaim Your Life.* Oakland, Calif.: New Harbinger.

Kabatznick, Ronna. 1998. *Zen of Eating: Ancient Answers to Modern Weight Problems.* New York: Berkeley.

May, Michelle, and Megrette Fletcher. 2012. *Eat What You Love, Love What You Eat with Diabetes.* Oakland, Calif.: New Harbinger.

Nhat Hanh, Thích, and Lilian Cheung. 2010. *Savor: Mindful Eating, Mindful Life.* New York: HarperOne.

Roth, Geneen. 2010. *Women, Food, and God: An Unexpected Path to Almost Everything.* New York: Scribner.

Tribole, Evelyn, and Elyse Resch. 2005. *Intuitive Eating: A Revolutionary Program That Works.* New York: St. Martin's Griffin.

Wansink, Brian. 2010. *Mindless Eating: Why We Eat More Than We Think.* New York: Bantam.

References

Baer, R. A. 2003. Mindfulness Training as a Clinical Intervention: A Conceptual and Empirical Review. *Clinical Psychology Science and Practice* 10: 125–143.

Baer, R. A., S. Fischer, and D. B. Huss. 2005. Mindfulness-Based Cognitive Therapy Applied to Binge Eating: A Case Study. *Cognitive and Behavioral Practice* 12: 351–358.

Bish, C. L., H. M. Blanck, M. K. Serdula, M. Marcus, H. W. Kohl III, and L. K Khan. 2005. Diet and Physical Activity Behaviors among Americans Trying to Lose Weight: 2000 Behavioral Risk Factor Surveillance System. *Obesity Research* March 13 (3): 596–607.

Christakis, N., and J. Fowler. 2007. The Spread of Obesity in a Large Social Network over 32 Years. *New England Journal of Medicine*. 357: 370–379.

Costin, C. 1999. *The Eating Disorder Sourcebook: A Comprehensive Guide to the Causes, Treatments, and Prevention of Eating Disorders*. Second edition. Los Angeles: Lowell House.

Dalen J., B. W. Smith, B. M. Shelley, A. L. Sloan, L. Leahigh, and D. Begay. 2010. Pilot Study: Mindful Eating and Living (MEAL): Weight, Eating Behavior, and Psychological Outcomes Associated with a Mindfulness-Based Intervention for People with Obesity. *Complementary Therapies in Medicine.* 18(6): 260–4.

Davidson, R. J., J. Kabat-Zinn, J. Schumacher, M. Rosenkrantz, D. Muller, S. F. Santorelli, et al. 2003. Alterations in Brain and Immune Function Produced by Mindfulness Meditation. *Psychosomatic Medicine* 65: 564–570.

Dennis, E. A., A. L. Dengo, D. L. Comber, K. D. Flack, J. Savla, K. P. Davy, and B. M. Davy. 2010. Water Consumption Increases Weight Loss During a Hypocaloric Diet Intervention in Middle-Aged and Older Adults. *Obesity* 18(2): 300–7.

Faude-Lang, V., M. Hartmann, E. M. Schmidt, P. Humpert , P. Nawroth, and W. Herzog. 2010. Acceptance- and Mindfulness-Based Group Intervention in Advanced Type 2 Diabetes Patients: Therapeutic Concept and Practical Experiences. *Psychotherapie, Psychosomatik, Medizinische Psychologie* 60(5): 185–9.

Flood-Obbagy, J. E., and B. J. Rolls. 2007. Soup Preloads in a Variety of Forms Reduce Meal Energy Intake. *Appetite* 49(3): 626–34.

Flood-Obbagy, J. E., and B. J. Rolls. 2009. The Effect of Fruit in Different Forms on Energy Intake and Satiety at a Meal. *Appetite* 52(2): 416–22.

Framson, C., A. R. Kristal, J. M. Schenk, A. J. Littman, S. Zeliadt, and D. Benitez. 2009. Development and Validation of the Mindful Eating Questionnaire. *Journal of the American Dietetic Association* 1439–1444.

Heatherton, T. F., and R. F. Baumeister. 1991. Binge Eating as Escape from Self-Awareness. *Psychological Bulletin* 110: 86–108.

Hetherington, M. M., A. S. Anderson, G. N. Norton, and L. Newson. 2006. Situational Effects on Meal Intake: A

Comparison of Eating Alone and Eating with Others. *Physiology & Behavior* July 30(4–5): 498–505.

Hetherington, M. M., and M. F. Regan. 2011. Effects of Chewing Gum on Short-Term Appetite Regulation in Moderately Restrained Eaters. *Appetite* 57(2): 475–82.

Hepworth, N. S. 2011. A Mindful Eating Group as an Adjunct to Individual Treatment for Eating Disorders: A Pilot Study. *Eating Disorders* 19(1): 6–16.

Higgs, S., and J. E. Donohoe. 2011. Focusing on Food During Lunch Enhances Lunch Memory and Decreases Later Snack Intake. *Appetite* 57(1): 202–06.

Higgs, S., and M. Woodward. 2009. Television Watching During Lunch Increases Afternoon Snack Intake of Young Women. *Appetite* 52(1): 39–43.

Honselman, C. S., J. E. Painter, K. J. Kennedy-Hagan, A. Halvorson, K. Rhodes, T. L. Brooks, and K. Skwir. 2011. In-Shell Pistachio Nuts Reduce Caloric Intake Compared to Shelled Nuts. *Appetite* 57(2): 414–17.

Kabat-Zinn, J. 1990. *Full Catastrophe Living: Using the Wisdom of Your Body and Mind to Face Stress, Pain, and Illness.* New York: Dell Publishing.

Kennedy-Hagan, K., J. E. Painter, C. Honselman, A. Halvorson, K. Rhodes, and K. Skwir. 2011. The Effect of Pistachio Shells as a Visual Cue in Reducing Caloric Consumption. *Appetite* 57(2): 418–20.

Kristal, A. R., A. J. Littman, D. Benitez, and E. White. 2005. Yoga Practice Is Associated with Attenuated Weight Gain in Healthy, Middle-Aged Men and Women. *Alternative Therapies in Health and Medicine* 11(4): 28–33.

Kristeller, J. L. 1999. An Exploratory Study of a Meditation-Based Intervention for Binge Eating Disorder. *Journal of Health Psychology* 4(3): 357–363.

Kristeller J. L., and R. Q. Wolever. 2011. Mindfulness-Based Eating Awareness Training for Treating Binge Eating Disorder: The Conceptual Foundation. *Eating Disorders* 19(1): 49–61.

Kruger, J., D. A. Galuska, M. K. Serdula, and D. A. Jones. 2004. Attempting to Lose Weight: Specific Practices among U.S. Adults. *American Journal of Preventive Medicine* June 26 (5): 402–06.

Lavender, J. M., B. F. Jardin, and D. A. Anderson. 2009. Bulimic Symptoms in Undergraduate Men and Women: Contributions of Mindfulness and Thought Suppression. *Eating Behavior* 10(4): 228–31.

McIver, S., M. McGartland, and P. O'Halloran. 2009. Overeating Is Not about the Food: Women Describe Their Experience of a Yoga Treatment Program for Binge Eating. *Qualitative Health Research* 19 (9): 1234–45.

Oldham-Cooper, R. E., C. A. Hardman, C. E. Nicoll, P. J. Rogers, and J. M. Brunstrom. 2011. Playing a Computer Game During Lunch Affects Fullness, Memory for Lunch, and Later Snack Intake. *American Journal of Clinical Nutrition* 93: 308–13.

Proulx, K. 2008. Experiences of Women with Bulimia Nervosa in a Mindfulness-Based Eating Disorder Treatment Group. *Eating Disorders* 16(1): 52–72.

Ramaekers, M. G., P. A. Luning, R. M. A. J. Ruijschop, C. M. M. Lakemond, and M. A. J. S. Van Boekel. 2001. Effect of Aroma Concentration and Exposure Time on Ad Libitum Soup Intake. *Appetite* 57(2): 542.

Rawal, A., J. Enayati, M. Williams, and R. Park. 2009. A mindful Approach to Eating Disorders. *Healthcare Counseling & Psychotherapy Journal* 9(4): 16–20.

Robinson, E. L., and S. Higgs. 2011. Memory and Food: Leaving the Best Till Last. *Appetite* 57(2): 538.

Rolls, B. J., L. S. Roe, and J. S. Meengs. 2004. Salad and Satiety: Energy Density and Portion Size of a First-Course Salad Affect Energy Intake at Lunch. *Journal of the American Dietetic Association* 104(10): 1570–06.

Rosenzweig, S., D. K. Reibel, J. M. Greeson, J. S. Edman, S. A. Jasser, K. D. McMearty, and B. J. Goldstein. 2007. Mindfulness-Based Stress Reduction Is Associated with Improved Glycemic Control in Type 2 Diabetes Mellitus: A Pilot Study. *Alternative Therapies in Health and Medicine* 13(5): 36–8.

Scisco, J. L., E. R. Muth, Y. Dong, A. W. Hoover. 2011. Slowing Bite-Rate Reduces Energy Intake: An Application of the Bite Counter Device. *Journal of the American Dietetic Association* 111(8): 1231–15.

Segal, Z., M. Williams, and J. Teasdale. 2001. *Mindfulness-Based Cognitive Therapy for Depression.* New York: Guilford Press.

Shimizu, M., Payne C. R., and B. Wansink. 2010. When Snacks Become Meals: How Hunger and Environmental Cues Bias Food Intake. *International Journal of Behavioral Nutrition and Physical Activity* 25, 7: 63.

Singh, N. N., G. E. Lancioni, A. N. Singh, A. S. W. Winton, J. Singh, K. M. McAleavey, A. D. Adkins, and S. D. S. Joy. 2008. A Mindfulness-Based Health Wellness Program for Managing Morbid Obesity. *Clinical Case Studies* 7(4): 327–339.

Smith, B. W., B. M. Shelley, L. Leahigh, and B. Vanleit. 2006. A Preliminary Study of the Effects of a Modified Mindfulness

Intervention on Binge Eating. *Complementary Health Practice Review* 11(3): 133–143.

Tantleff-Dunn, S., R. D. Barnes, and J. G. Larose. 2011. It's Not Just a "Woman Thing": The Current State of Normative Discontent. *Eating Disorders* 19(5): 392–402.

Tapper, K., C. Shaw, J. Ilsley, A. J. Hill, F. W. Bond, and L. Moore. 2009. Exploratory Randomised Controlled Trial of a Mindfulness-Based Weight Loss Intervention for Women. *Appetite* 52 (2): 396–404.

Timmerman, G. M., and A. Brown. 2012. The effect of a mindful restaurant eating intervention on weight management in women. *Journal of Nutritional Education and Behavior* 44(1): 22–28.

van Son, J. I. Nyklíček, V. J. Pop, and F. Pouwer. 2011. Testing the Effectiveness of a Mindfulness-Based Intervention to Reduce Emotional Distress in Outpatients with Diabetes (Diamind): Design of a Randomized Controlled Trial. *BMC Public Health* February 24: 131.

Wansink, B., and J. Sobal. 2007. Mindless Eating: The 200 Daily Food Decisions We Overlook. *Environment and Behavior* 39(1): 106–23.

C. Martha Stutzman

Susan Albers, PsyD, is a psychologist at the Cleveland Clinic Family Health Center who specializes in eating issues, weight loss, body image concerns, and mindfulness. After obtaining masters and doctorate degrees from the University of Denver, Albers completed an internship at the University of Notre Dame in South Bend, IN, and a post-doctoral fellowship at Stanford University. She conducts mindful eating workshops across the United States and internationally.

Albers is author of *50 Ways to Soothe Yourself Without Food; Eat, Drink, and Be Mindful; Mindful Eating 101,* and *But I Deserve This Chocolate!* Her work has been featured in many media publications including *O, the Oprah Magazine; Shape; Prevention; Vanity Fair;* and the *Wall Street Journal,* and she blogs for the *Huffington Post* and *Psychology Today.* Albers has been a featured expert on many radio and television shows, including *Dr. Oz* and various programs on CNN and NPR.

A member of the Academy for Eating Disorders and the International Association of Eating Disorder Professionals, she enjoys blogging, jogging, watching the Sundance Channel, and traveling. Visit Susan Albers online at www.eatingmindfully.com.

Foreword writer **Lilian Cheung, DSc, RD,** is a lecturer and director of health promotion and communication in the department of nutrition at the Harvard School of Public Health. She is a coinvestigator at the Harvard Prevention Research Center on Nutrition and Physical Activity, cocreator of the school-based program, *Eat Well & Keep Moving,* and founder and editorial director of The Nutrition Source website, www.thenutritionsource.org. Cheung is also coauthor of *Be Healthy! It's a Girl Thing,* and *Savor: Mindful Eating, Mindful Life.* www.savorthebook.com